# stand

## CORE TRUTHS YOU MUST KNOW
## FOR AN UNSHAKABLE FAITH

# ALEX McFARLAND

TYNDALE

**Tyndale House Publishers, Inc.**
**Wheaton, Illinois**

ISBN: 1-58997-353-4

A Focus on the Family book published by
Tyndale House Publishers, Wheaton, Illinois 60189

*TYNDALE* is a registered trademark of Tyndale House Publishers, Inc. Tyndale's
quill logo is a trademark of Tyndale House Publishers, Inc.

All Scripture quotations, unless otherwise indicated, are taken from the *Holy Bible,
New International Version*®. NIV®. Copyright © 1973, 1978, 1984 by International
Bible Society. Used by permission of Zondervan Publishing House. All rights
reserved. Scripture quotations marked (KJV) are taken from the *King James Version*.
Scripture quotations marked (NKJV) are taken from the *New King James Version*.
Copyright © 1982 by Thomas Nelson, Inc. Used by permission. All rights reserved.
Scripture quotations marked (NASB) are taken from the *New American Standard
Bible*®. Copyright © The Lockman Foundation 1960, 1962, 1963, 1968, 1971,
1972, 1973, 1975, 1977, 1995. Used by permission. (www.Lockman.org). Scripture
quotations marked (MSG) are taken from *The Message*. Copyright © by Eugene H.
Peterson 1993, 1994, 1995. Used by permission of NavPress Publishing Group.

The names of some of the people in this book and the details surrounding their
stories have been changed to protect their privacy.

Editor: Marianne K. Hering
Cover copy: Carol Hubbard
Cover design: Kurt Birky

Library of Congress Cataloging-in-Publication Data
McFarland, Alex, 1964-
  Stand : core truths you must know for an unshakable faith / Alex
McFarland.
      p. cm. — (Focus on the Family)
  Includes bibliographical references.
  ISBN 1-58997-353-4
  1. Jesus Christ--Person and offices—Biblical teaching. 2. Theology, Doctrinal—
Popular works. I. Title. II. Focus on the Family presents.
  BT203.M339 2005
  232'.8—dc22
                                        2005017146

Printed in the United States of America
1 2 3 4 5 6 7 8 9 /10 09 08 07 06 05

This book is gratefully dedicated to

NLG
GRH
HLW
JDM
JLF

from whom I learned very much.
Thank you.

*This is what the LORD says: "**Stand** at the crossroads and look; ask for the ancient paths, ask where the good way is, and walk in it, and you will find rest for your souls."*

—JEREMIAH 6:16

# Contents

# Acknowledgments

The following people have not only helped to make this book a reality but have shaped my life deeply.

To Mike Umlandt, who helped me format and clarify this work.

Special thanks are due to the wonderful team that is Focus on the Family. This includes my boss and friend, Bob Waliszewski. Also Larry Weeden, Clark Miller, Tom Neven, Marianne Hering, Bruce Peppin, Rebecca Hofland, Brian Merculief, and everyone at Global Resources, Briargate Media, Peak Creative, and so many more.

The wonderful people and churches of Greensboro, North Carolina, and the Piedmont area have stood with me since I began my apologetics work in the mid-1990s. Thank you. For their support in the early days of my apologetics/worldview ministry through the 50-States-in-50-Days "Tour of Truth" to the "Truth for a New Generation" events and simulcasts, I am forever indebted to dear friends throughout the United States. I offer thanks overflowing to the Vance H. Havner Scholarship Board, the people of Pleasant Garden Baptist Church, and also to Lydia Bowman, Peggy Rice, and Bert Stokes.

Very special appreciation is extended to Stuart Epperson Jr. of "Truth Talk Live" radio and also to Tom Booth and David Parsons. Thanks go out to Carla McGlynn/Planet Travel, John Beasley of Professional Video Services, Keith Deltano/Freedom Entertainment, Marty Dupree/BSCNC, and to Toby Frost/

NAMB. Very special love and appreciation go out to Jeffrey Foskett of the Brian Wilson Band.

Sincere appreciation is given to those people who have helped me stand firm in my faith whom I may have failed to mention on these pages.

I thank the Lord for Christian parents, Neill and Becky McFarland; for Anne Lowe, my godly mother-in-law; and for beloved family members who lift me up in prayer.

My steadfast love and devotion are forever given to my wife, Angie. I could not imagine a wife who does more for both Savior and spouse.

I am thankful for the Bible, which for 20 years has been an ever-present friend.

Most of all, I am grateful for the Lord Jesus Christ, who loved me and gave Himself for me.

# ONE

# How to Understand the Core Truths of Christianity

*Much dreaming and many words are meaningless.*
*Therefore **stand** in awe of God.*

—ECCLESIASTES 5:7

It all started with a green baseball cap.

My friend Mike was wearing it when Professor Harley saw the Bible reference embroidered on the hat—John 3:16. The effect was like waving a red flag in front of a bull.

"Anyone who believes in that Bible crud is a complete idiot," Dr. Harley said.

Kind and gentle Mike didn't know how to respond to such a hostile comment. Additionally, the professor had a reputation for tying Christians up in philosophical knots. So the next day Mike asked me to meet the college professor and talk with him about why the Bible is true.

I went gladly.

"I'm warning you, Alex, this guy *hates* Christianity," Mike said when we arrived at the professor's house.

Mike was right. As soon as I walked in the door this 40-year-old man with a long, gray ponytail and wearing a Carhartt jacket bragged, "Give me 30 minutes with any preacher and I can make him doubt that God even exists."

*Was that a hello?*

"This is my friend I was telling you about," Mike said to Dr. Harley, trying to restore politeness.

"It's nice to meet you," I said to the professor, extending my hand for a greeting.

The professor ignored the offer of a handshake and then looked me over, sizing me up. "Give me a couple of hours and I can turn any Christian into an atheist. Even you."

In 15 years of teaching the Bible and speaking hundreds of times throughout America, I had never met someone so openly angry and rude. I smiled at the professor and said, "Well, you and the devil are in the same business." I let that sink in, then added, "He's just faster."

"What do you mean?"

"In the Garden of Eden, Satan convinced Adam and Eve to doubt God," I explained. "Satan turned them into doubters and agnostics, but it took him only a couple of minutes—"

"So you believe that Genesis stuff," the professor cut in. "Well, this tells me a lot about what kind of Christian I am talking to!"

For the next couple of hours we sat in his home office and talked. Regardless of the conversation topic, the professor kept knocking down Christianity and its followers, calling them "ignorant, uninformed, simpleminded believers." With just as much determination I kept reminding the professor about the reality of Jesus and of Jesus' love for him personally.

At one point, I leaned across the desk looking him directly in the eyes. "Dr. Harley," I said, "you are obviously very intelligent, highly educated, and you say you're an atheist. So doesn't it strike

## Why Study the Bible and Its Doctrines?

1. It is one of God's homework assignments to Christians (2 Timothy 2:15).

2. Knowledge of the Bible helps a person resist sin (Psalm 119:9-11).

3. Believers are told to "contend for the faith" (Jude 3). You must understand the faith before you can present, explain, or defend it (see also 1 Peter 3:15).

4. Jesus commanded believers to study the Bible, because He is its theme (see John 5:39, Luke 24:27).

5. Believers who were known for their study of the Bible get complimented in the New Testament (see Acts 17:10-11).

6. In a world full of error, the Bible is the reliable source of truth (see John 17:17, Psalm 119:142).

7. The Bible provides necessary spiritual nourishment, changing our lives for the better (see Matthew 4:4).

8. Attitude toward God's Word is an indicator of one's love for God's Son (see John 14:15).

9. It is promised that the author of the Bible (the Holy Spirit) will come alongside to teach and tutor the reader (1 John 2:27).

you as odd that for two hours I've listened to you talk about someone who doesn't exist?"

As we continued to talk, my heart went out to this well-educated but misguided man. Finally his soul opened up, and Dr. Harley shared with Mike and me how some unpleasant church experiences as a teenager led him to have doubts about God and then disbelief in the Bible. He dealt with his hurt and anger by trying to squash the faith of other people.

"Okay," I said, "you say there is no God, no afterlife, and we all just die, rot back into the soil, and that's it. Right?"

"Science proves it!" he said.

"Let me ask you something kind of personal. Deep down, do you hope your view is true? I mean, are you glad that this is how things are?"

His answer was surprising. "No one's ever asked me that before. I don't know. Not really. My mother was a Christian. I'd like to think that one day I'll see her again, but that's just false hope. I can't lower myself to accept some primitive Christian beliefs."

As Mike and I walked out the door, the professor said some things that have stuck with me: "In a way, I'm envious of people who can have faith. But what I can't understand are those Christians who never learn anything about what they say they believe. If I ever did convert, I would learn everything possible about God."

## Why It's Important to Know Your Stuff

The professor had a point. Many Christians do not know why they believe or what they believe. Not long ago, a survey of "born again Christians" by the Barna Research Group concluded that Christians are often ignorant about their faith. Even though 98 percent of those surveyed said that their Christian faith is very important in their life, some of the survey's findings were discouraging. For example:

- Thirty-eight percent believe that if a person is generally good he can earn a place in heaven. (This contradicts the Bible, which says eternal life is "the gift of God"; see Romans 6:23, Titus 3:5, Ephesians 2:8-9.)
- Fifty percent said that Satan is "not a living being but is a symbol of evil." (The Bible clearly identifies Satan as a living being, calling him "your enemy"; see 1 Peter 5:8.)
- Thirty-one percent of born again Christians agree with the statement "While He lived on earth, Jesus committed sins, like other people."[1] (The Bible says that Jesus was perfect; He never sinned; see Hebrews 4:14-15.)

In a world of psychic hotlines, horoscopes, Wicca, and alternative spirituality, Christians must be able to share their beliefs effectively. When a friend has a question about God, the Christian should have an answer. The Bible commands us to know our beliefs so that we will be equipped to represent our Lord (see 2 Timothy 2:15, also 2 Timothy 3:14-17).

Not only that, but Christians who don't know why they believe what they believe are in spiritual danger. Many people who join cults and nonbiblical religious groups once claimed to be Christians. Several years ago I interviewed a former cult leader on a radio program.

The man explained that of the 200 people who joined his

religious organization each month, virtually all of the new recruits had been at one time members of churches.

"We were growing in people and taking in lots of money," the former cult leader explained. "I didn't want to rock the boat, but secretly, I could never understand how all these church people didn't see that our beliefs were exactly opposite, you know, incompatible."

Our radio interview continued, and by the end of the broadcast my heart was heavy. The man said something that made the evangelist in me really sad:

> People gave different reasons for leaving the church, for getting into alternative spiritualities, like us. Some people were fed up with church cliques, and others were burned out on church conflict. But most were just people searching for answers, and they had no understanding of what Christianity was really about. They couldn't see the discrepancy between the false and the true. We [the cult leaders] used to brag that we basically took in an entire church of ex-Christians each month.[2]

It is time that we Christians get a solid grasp on Christianity. This book is about six core truths that are taught in the Bible and are central to Christianity. Knowledge of Bible truths is crucial for personal growth and for Christian service. God has given believers throughout history the special job of sharing Christ with their own generation. But to do this, we have to have a solid understanding of the message we are presenting.

Beyond that, it only makes sense that a Christian would want to have a strong knowledge about this faith in which he has entrusted his soul. Through personal experience and in teaching biblical truth to others, I have seen that learning about the core truths of Christianity leads believers to a stronger relationship with God and passion to tell others about Jesus Christ.

## The Bible Is Relevant Today

"I never knew that this Bible stuff would really be so . . . well, interesting." When a teenager said that to me at an event where I had spoken, I thanked him for making my day.

People sometimes assume that deep, detailed Bible study will be boring. They struggle to see how events that happened centuries ago are relevant to their lives today. Maybe they were made to sit through too many monotonous sermons. I guess a lackluster presentation could make any subject seem dull. But think again before you assume that the content of Scripture is dull or irrelevant. Verses like Psalm 119:93 express the wonderful and lasting impact that come from understanding the Bible:

> I will never forget Your precepts,
> For by them You have given me life. (NKJV)

## The Real Deal

Several years ago when I was still in school, I saw some Izod shirts at the mall—you know, the sharp-looking tennis shirts with the little alligator emblem. I really wanted one, but in the big department store they were kind of expensive. *If they ever go on sale,* I thought, *I'm going to buy one.*

Fast-forward a couple of weeks. I saw a TV commercial that

promised a big sale with "Computers! Stereos! Household items! Clothing! And more! All at unbelievable prices!" I was convinced—these deals were too good to miss.

At the big sale I was pleased to see a rack of Izod shirts. There were dozens of them in every color you could imagine. I couldn't believe my good fortune. Izods at a discount meant I could afford to buy two.

I was so proud of my new Izod shirts that I wore them almost every day for over a week. Monday was green shirt day, Tuesday I wore the yellow shirt. Wear and wash, wash and wear. I went to school feeling stylish every day.

Two weeks later I was putting on one of my new shirts when I noticed that the snazzy little alligator emblem had fallen off. In a hurry, I yelled downstairs, "Mom, is my yellow Izod clean?" As I was putting on my "good" shirt, an amazing thing happened. One sleeve of the yellow shirt fell off. I stared in disbelief

> "Christians don't necessarily need to hear a lot of new things; they just need to be reminded of some important old things."
> —ANONYMOUS

at my precious, less-than-two-weeks-old designer shirt with a sleeve hanging by only a thread. Now the green shirt with the missing alligator looked pretty good. Discouraged that my trendy shirts were falling apart, I rushed off to a family reunion.

At the picnic, I saw my brother-in-law David, who happens to work in the textile industry. I told him about the shirts.

"Let me take a look at the tag in the back of your shirt," David said.

He let go of the tag he was reading, turned me around, and said, "These are not authentic Izod shirts. We see it all the time in textiles. What you bought are cheap imitations, and that's why they are coming apart. Alex, you've been ripped off."

Things began to make sense, and I began to feel pretty foolish. How could elite designer shirts have been priced so inexpensively? And why would exclusive shirts like this be among the odd assortment of items at a big

> *"Knowledge of Scripture is knowledge of Christ, and ignorance of them is ignorance of Him."*
> —JEROME (A.D. 340-420)[3]

warehouse sale? This was my first exposure to knockoffs: fake, look-alike products. After another washing, the shirts completely fell apart, and so did my feeling of having scored a good deal.

## Authenticity Is Key

Buying phony knockoff shirts was a disappointment, costing me just a little more than $20. But trusting in a false Savior would be more than disappointing—it would be disastrous. The cost would be beyond calculation. The value of your soul and the length of eternity are clear reminders of the importance of believing *truth*.

We live in a world where millions of people embrace thousands of belief systems. Yet Jesus said that there is only one way for someone to enter heaven—by being "born again" through Jesus Christ (see John 3:3, 14:6). (We'll discuss this more in chapter 5.)

Millions of people do not have a clear understanding of what it means to be a Christian. And even many who are Christians can't give a basic explanation about what they believe.

Mordecai Hamm was a Jewish man who became a much talked about Christian leader. Hamm was passionate in his belief that every believer should know the core truths of the Bible and share them with others. He saw this not as a chore, but as each Christian's privilege. Hamm enthusiastically declared:

> No option, no alibi, no excuse! Every Christian has an obligation to a lost world![4]

In the course of his travels, Hamm taught one young man about the core truth of salvation through Jesus Christ. This most famous convert was Billy Graham, who would eventually preach to more people than anyone else in history—210 million people.[5]

One person, standing on God's truth, can make a difference. Let's look at six core truths that will make a difference in your life.

### Lost in Translations

If you walk into a well-stocked Bible bookstore, you'll find at least 20 different versions of the Bible. A person could get lost in rows and rows of different types of Bibles. Some of the common ones are the *King James Version*, the *New International Version*, *The Message*, the *New American Standard Bible*, and the *Revised Standard Version*. In books with Bible verses quoted, the different translations are sometimes marked with tiny little initials that look like this: KJV, NIV, MSG, NASB, or RSV.

Why so many translations? A single word in Hebrew or Greek, the original languages of the Bible, can mean many different things. In English, a good example would be the word *deep*. A "deep" thought would not be translated in the same way as a "deep" swimming pool or a "deep" blue jacket. A translator would have to think of the best way to communicate the concept of "deep" as it is used in a particular context.

As a result, whenever the Bible is translated into English, translators sometimes choose different English words to represent the Hebrew or Greek concepts. Modern translations use more modern words and different translation theories than the first English version, which was translated 600 years ago.

Consider these three different versions of Philippians 2:3:

> Let nothing be done through strife or vainglory; but in lowliness of mind let each esteem other better than themselves. (KJV)

> Do nothing out of selfish ambition or vain conceit, but in humility consider others better than yourselves. (NIV)

> Don't push your way to the front; don't sweet-talk your way to the top. Put yourself aside, and help others get ahead. (MSG)

They all say the same thing, just in a different style and with different vocabulary. Rest assured that no matter which mainstream Bible you buy, the essence of the gospel remains the same: Jesus is alive!

# TWO

# Core Truth 1: Inspiration

## Christians Believe the Bible Was Written by God Through Men

*"The word of our God **stands** forever."*

—Isaiah 40:8

Unshakable faith begins with the Bible.

The Christian faith is only as certain as the Bible is trustworthy. If the Bible isn't true, then people who call themselves Christians would have no truth to stand on—their faith would be worthless.

Is your faith based on truth? How can you know for sure?

For hundreds of years people who reject Christianity have attacked the Bible. Their thinking goes like this: If they can prove that the Bible is not an accurate account of God's work in history, they can then say it's not true. If they can say the Bible isn't true, they can then reject the claims that Jesus is God, that Jesus died on the cross for our sins, and that Jesus arose from the dead. If they can prove the Bible isn't true, they can say Christians are just misguided people. If they can prove the Bible isn't true, they can say Jesus' resurrection—the most important event that Christianity is based on—never happened.

*If* they can prove it—but they can't.

For hundreds of years the Bible's critics—all of them—have failed. Still, they try.

*The Da Vinci Code* is one of the most recent efforts to cast doubt on the Bible's truth. The best-selling novel by Dan Brown mixes historical fact with fiction to confuse people about the authenticity of the Bible, in particular the first four books of the New Testament that chronicle the life of Christ. These are called the Gospels, and the books are Matthew, Mark, Luke, and John. The author of *The Da Vinci Code* attacks the New Testament through a fictional main character, Leigh Teabing. Teabing is a royal historian who claims, "Almost everything our fathers taught us about Christ is *false*."[1] Teabing goes on to explain that it's because at an important church meeting, the Council of Nicea in the year 325, Roman Emperor Constantine "commissioned and financed a new Bible" that "embellished" the Gospels to make Christ more godlike.

Is *The Da Vinci Code* right? Did church leaders in A.D. 325 make up parts of the Gospels?

No, and no!

The Council of Nicea is an actual event in history, but there's no evidence that church leaders agreed to change Scripture to fit a desired doctrine or teaching. On the contrary, at Nicea church leaders affirmed the clear teaching of the Gospels written more than two centuries earlier: Jesus Christ is God.

Since *The Da Vinci Code* was published, however, I've talked to many teens who aren't sure they can trust their Bible. They're asking questions like "Is it true that man wrote the Bible hundreds of years after Jesus lived? Did people really fight over what the Bible was going to say? I mean, what if the things that ended up in the Bible weren't what God really *meant* the Bible to say?"

## The Bible Was Written by God Through Men

To answer those questions and others like them, let's start our discovery of Christianity's core truths with what the Bible says about itself. In verse after verse, more than 3,000 in all, the Bible claims to be the actual words of God.

Here are two key references in the New Testament:

Above all, you must understand that no prophecy of
Scripture came about by the prophet's own interpretation.
For prophecy never had its origin in the will of man, but
men spoke from God as they were carried along by the
Holy Spirit. (2 Peter 1:20-21)

All Scripture is God-breathed and is useful for teaching,
rebuking, correcting and training in righteousness.
(2 Timothy 3:16)

The Bible makes an impressive claim about itself—it says it is written by God through men. That's what Bible scholars mean by **inspiration**. The Bible didn't just plop down from heaven in a deluxe leather cover. Humans were very much involved, "carried along by the Holy Spirit," said Peter, one of Jesus' followers and a key leader of the church. Men wrote as God guided them, not making up their own message. The words they wrote were "God-breathed," which is the meaning of "inspired." All of Scripture is inspired, breathed out from the mouth of God, so to speak.

I used to think this meant that God dictated exactly what He wanted the Bible to say to the humans who diligently wrote it down word for word. But after a number of years of reading and studying all of Scripture, I know that's not how most of the Bible was written.

Sometimes God did dictate exactly what to write, as when God gave Moses the exact wording of the Ten Commandments (Exodus 20) and even engraved the words on stone tablets (Exodus 32:16). Usually, however, the Bible displays a human and divine partnership—the Holy Spirit working through the writer's personality and creativity to express the words of God.

Even when the biblical writers state clearly that God was directing them, the words they write reflect their unique personality and place in history. For example, God gave an unpleasant task to the prophet Jeremiah. He got to announce to the Israelites (God's people who would become known as the Jews) that they would be dragged off to the land of Babylonia for 70 years. Jeremiah wrote:

> Then the LORD reached out his hand and touched my mouth and said to me, "Now, I have put my words in your mouth. See, today I appoint you over nations and kingdoms to uproot and tear down, to destroy and overthrow, to build and to plant."
>
> The word of the LORD came to me: "What do you see, Jeremiah?"

"I see the branch of an almond tree," I replied.

The LORD said to me, "You have seen correctly, for I am watching to see that my word is fulfilled."

The word of the LORD came to me again: "What do you see?"

"I see a boiling pot, tilting away from the north," I answered.

The LORD said to me, "From the north disaster will be poured out on all who live in the land. I am about to summon all the peoples of the northern kingdoms," declares the LORD. (Jeremiah 1:9-15)

This pattern is repeated throughout the book of Jeremiah with the prophet writing over and over: "This is what the LORD says . . ." "Hear what the LORD says . . ." "Then the word of the LORD came to me . . ."

Another Old Testament prophet, Isaiah, wrote a much different book, one filled with some of the Bible's most beautiful poetry:

Comfort, comfort my people, says your God. Speak tenderly to Jerusalem, and proclaim to her that her hard service has been completed, that her sin has been paid for, that she has received from the LORD's hand double for all her sins.

A voice of one calling:
"In the desert prepare
     the way for the LORD;
make straight in the wilderness
     a highway for our God.
Every valley shall be raised up,

every mountain and hill made low;
the rough ground shall become level,
   the rugged places a plain.
And the glory of the LORD will be revealed,
   and all mankind together will see it. For the mouth of
     the LORD has spoken."
A voice says, "Cry out."
   And I said, "What shall I cry?"
"All men are like grass,
   and all their glory is like the flowers of the field.
The grass withers and the flowers fall,
   because the breath of the LORD blows on them.
   Surely the people are grass.
The grass withers and the flowers fall,
   but the word of our God **stands** forever." (Isaiah
     40:1-8, emphasis added)

Like Jeremiah and Isaiah, the other Old Testament writers believed they were putting down God's words, described as "perfect" and "trustworthy" in Psalm 19:7. Perhaps most important, God's word has no expiration date:

The word of our God **stands** forever. (Isaiah 40:8, emphasis added)

Your word, O LORD, is eternal; it **stands** firm in the heavens. (Psalm 119:89, emphasis added)

How about the New Testament writers? The apostle Paul contributed letters that make up a large part of the New Testament. He had a miraculous encounter with Jesus and became a dynamic preacher and pastor. Paul wrote, "This is what we speak, not in words taught us by human wisdom but in words taught by the Spirit" (1 Corinthians 2:13).

## Jesus and the Old and New Testaments

We've looked at what the Bible says about itself. But another important perspective should also be considered: What did Jesus say about the Scriptures?

When Jesus spoke about "the Law of Moses, the Prophets and the Psalms" (Luke 24:44), listeners in His day knew what He meant—all of the Hebrew Scriptures. Today those books are known as the Old Testament. Jesus would have known about them because the last book of the Old Testament, Malachi, was written about 400 years before He was born.

What Jesus had to say about the Bible is very important because He is the all-knowing God of truth. (See the box "What Jesus Said About the Scriptures.") The Bible teaches that Jesus is the Son of God, the Lord Almighty who came to earth in human form. (We will explain why Jesus is God in chapter 4.) When Jesus quoted from the Hebrew Scriptures, He validated their truth and verified their accuracy. He also looked ahead to the truthful recording of the New Testament.

Near the end of His ministry on earth, just hours before He would die on the cross, Jesus made an important twofold promise to His disciples:

> "All this I have spoken while still with you. But the Counselor, the Holy Spirit, whom the Father will send in my

name, will teach you all things and will remind you of everything I have said to you." (John 14:25-26)

Jesus was speaking to 11 of the men who had been with Him throughout His three-year ministry, men who had witnessed everything He had done. Now He was entrusting His ministry to them. "And you also must testify, for you have been with me from the beginning" (John 15:27).

But they would not be left on their own. Jesus promised that the Holy Spirit "will teach you all things and will remind you of everything I have said to you." When it came time to recording God's message, the New Testament authors recognized that they

### What Jesus Said About the Scriptures

- "I tell you the truth, until heaven and earth disappear, not the smallest letter, not the least stroke of a pen, will by any means disappear from the Law until everything is accomplished." (Matthew 5:18)
- "Heaven and earth will pass away, but my words will never pass away." (Matthew 24:35, Mark 13:31)
- "It is easier for heaven and earth to disappear than for the least stroke of a pen to drop out of the Law." (Luke 16:17)
- "Everything must be fulfilled that is written about me in the Law of Moses, the Prophets and the Psalms." (Luke 24:44)
- "The Scripture cannot be broken." (John 10:35)

were writing Scripture—that they were, in fact, conveying God's truth as the Spirit of God gave it to them.

## The Evidence for Inspiration

Some people today have one basic belief about the Bible—that it should not be believed! But it didn't used to be that way. Prior to the late twentieth century, virtually all people who claimed to be Christians had understood Scripture to be inspired and preserved—in other words, sacred. They believed God had given us His Word and that these Scriptures were to be followed. The Bible is supposed to judge us, but some people would like to judge the Bible instead.

But the Bible is trustworthy, and that trustworthiness begins with the core truth of **inspiration**: The Bible was written by God through men.

Many skeptics have pointed out, however, that the Bible is not proven to be God's Word just because some of its verses say so. We come back to the questions raised by *The Da Vinci Code*: "Is it true that man wrote the Bible hundreds of years after Jesus lived? Did people really fight over what the Bible was going to say? I mean, what if the things that ended up in the Bible weren't what God really *meant* the Bible to say?"

Christians have ready answers, though, because the Bible's divine origin is indicated by some very compelling evidence.

### *Evidence 1: It Has Been Preserved and Is Indestructible*
It's been banned, burned, and banished for centuries, but the Bible has outlived all of its enemies. The Roman Emperor Diocletian, for example, ordered all Bibles destroyed in A.D. 303.

Though his attempt to purge the world of Bibles was fervent, only 20 years later Emperor Constantine offered a reward for any remaining Bibles. Within 24 hours, more than 50 complete copies were brought before him.[2]

Not too long ago the Soviet dictator Joseph Stalin sought to establish a completely secular, godless state. In late 1920s, he ordered that all Bibles be purged from the Soviet Union.[3] But as communism fell and the Soviet Union dissolved, a 1980s poll showed that a greater percentage of Soviet citizens than ever believed that the Bible is the Word of God.

The fact that millions of people today can hold a Bible in their hands and hide its words in their hearts, after centuries of attack and opposition, is evidence of the Bible's divine origin. God has preserved His Word; it cannot be destroyed.

To better understand how the Bible has been preserved, we need to look at the oldest manuscripts—what is called the manuscript evidence. The core truth of **inspiration** means God gave us His Word exactly as He wanted, without error. But only the original documents were inspired, and we don't have those original copies. So how do we know that the Bible we read today is an accurate and trustworthy copy of the original writings?

We have confidence in our copies of the Bible because research indicates that the Bible's content has been accurately passed down through the centuries.

Over hundreds of years, thousands of copies of the individual books that make up the Bible have been discovered. Some ancient manuscripts of the Old Testament date back to before the birth of Jesus. Scholars and historians who have studied these ancient manuscripts—written by hand before the days of the printing press and photocopy machine—have continually been impressed at the careful way the text of the Bible was transmitted without change.

Consider how the Jewish people of old handled the Hebrew Scriptures, our Old Testament. The books of "the Law of Moses, the Prophets and the Psalms" were carefully copied on leather sheets (and later on papyrus, a type of paper made from reeds). Scribes were a special group of people whose job in life was to copy and copy and copy the Holy Word of the Lord. The word *scribe* literally means "counter."[4] As a scribe copied Scripture, the letters on each page would actually be counted—forward and backward—on the master copy and on the new rendition to ensure nothing was added and nothing omitted. Can you say *migraine*? Because of the scribes' hard work and devotion, we have accurate copies of the Bible today.

Additionally, scholars say that even if none of the 5,500 ancient New Testament manuscripts existed, the whole text of the 27 books could be recovered. How is that? The entire New Testament—Matthew through Revelation—could be known from quotations of verses found in the writings and letters of early Christians.[5] One scholar, Hans von Kampenhausen, said:

The New Testament meets all the demands of historical reliability that could possibly be made of such a text. If the New Testament were any other book, its authenticity would be regarded beyond all doubt.[6]

F. F. Bruce, a renowned scholar from Manchester, England, stated:

The evidence for our New Testament writings is ever so much greater than the evidence for many writings of other classical authors—the authenticity of which no one dreams of questioning. . . . If the New Testament had been a collection of secular writings, their authenticity would generally be regarded as beyond all doubt.[7]

Bruce was pointing out that a different standard of judgment has been applied to the New Testament than has been applied to any other ancient writings. The New Testament exists in thousand of copies, dating from a period very close to the actual events it covers. Historians note that the New Testament appears to have been carefully copied and widely circulated. If there were discrepancies, contradictions, or alterations, the early Christians easily could have recognized and pointed them out. It is not for lack of evidence that skeptics discount the accuracy of the Bible.

There's another aspect of the Bible's preservation we need to consider: Who decided on the books to include in the "canon of Scripture," and when? In part because of *The Da Vinci Code*, this topic of canonicity is a fairly hot topic of conversation. Some false beliefs have almost reached urban legend status, namely that some books in the Bible—the Gospels—were changed by people with evil motives and that other documents were hidden away.

Hear this: **Such doubt and speculation have no support from history.**

In fact, the manner in which the Bible books were carefully preserved is an inspiring story in itself. Men did not randomly choose which books would be called Scripture. The copying and circulation of the Bible did take place with amazing speed for the period of time we are talking about—nearly 2,000 years ago. But in an age before printing presses, electricity, and mass communication, it took some time before most of the people who desired God's Word had access to it.

### *Evidence 2: There Is Unity to the Bible*

The entire Bible was written by about 40 individuals over 1,500 years. These writers included a farmer (Amos), a doctor (Luke), ministers (such as Ezra and James), political leaders (David, Solomon), political prisoners (Daniel, John), a musician (Asaph), a fisherman (Peter), and a tax collector (Matthew).

Moses, who wrote the first five books of the Old Testament, grew up wealthy in Egypt, became a fugitive, worked herding livestock, and eventually led a nation. Paul, who wrote 13 books of the New Testament, was professionally trained in religion, theology, and philosophy, and before he became a Christian led a movement to hunt down the followers of Jesus Christ. The Bible writers were rich and educated, poor and not-so-educated; they came from a wide variety of social backgrounds.

Yet the Bible contains a unified, consistent message. It could be summarized as "God's Savior, and how you may know Him" or "The kingdom of heaven, and how to get in."

The agreement among all 66 books strongly argues in favor of the Bible's heavenly origin. Though humans did the writing, the Bible is really the product of one author—God.

Churches and Christians did not choose the books they wanted to put in the Bible. They eventually recognized the books that God had chosen. Bible expert J. I. Packer wrote:

The church no more "gave us" the canon than Sir Isaac Newton "gave us" the force of gravity. God gave us gravity by the work of His creation, and similarly, He gave us the New Testament canon by inspiring the original books that make it up.[8]

What is meant by the word *canon*? (No, not something on a pirate ship that shoots bowling balls—that's a ca*nn*on.) Scholars use the term *canon* when referring to the 66 books of the Bible. In ancient times, the Latin word *canon* meant "measuring stick." The "Canon of Scripture" is the group of manuscripts that make up the Bible. These writings were carefully copied, preserved, and collected together. Dedicated Christians spent much time and prayer in carefully assembling the books that God had given as His Word. Tests for "canonicity" included considerations such as: ***Authorship*** (Who wrote the book?); ***acceptance by churches*** (Was the book's content generally embraced or rejected?); ***acceptance by recognized leaders*** (Did the men who had been with Jesus or did the Christians who had spent time with Jesus' disciples accept the book?); ***spiritual value*** (Is the content of the book in question useful, profitable, beneficial for believers, individually and collectively?) During the early church era, there were also writings in circulation that Christians recognized were not from God, and they were *rejected* for canonization.

### Evidence 3: The Bible Is Supported by Archaeology
Though the Bible is not purely a history book, the events and people recorded in its pages are historical. Over the past couple of centuries, the science of archaeology has advanced our knowledge of the people, places, and culture of Bible times. In the

process, archaeology has proved, over and over again, that the Bible is accurate in its historical facts.

For example, proof of King Jehu (see 2 Kings 9–10) was discovered on an obelisk (a column of stone) found in 1846. The obelisk contains words and pictures recording Israel's conquest by an Assyrian king. The obelisk's information perfectly confirms what was recorded in the Old Testament. Other than what is in the Bible, little information has been found about the ancient kings of Israel, but obelisk discoveries mesh perfectly with the Bible's account. We can trust what the Bible has recorded about the ancient activities of the Jewish people.

### Evidence 4: The Bible Has Fulfilled Prophecy

Fulfilled prophecy distinguishes the Bible from any other religious book. The Bible could accurately predict events hundreds of years in advance because God was the author.

Sometime between A.D. 30-32, Jesus predicted that the Jewish

---

**What the Believer Should Do for the Bible**

- Desire it (1 Peter 2:2)
- Read it (Deuteronomy 31:11, Luke 4:16, Colossians 3:16)
- Obey it (Psalm 119:9, 1 Timothy 4:16, Matthew 4:4)
- Present it to others (Matthew 28:19-20, 2 Timothy 4:2)
- Correctly understand it (2 Timothy 2:15)
- Suffer and, if necessary, die for it (Revelation 1:9, 6:9, 20:4)

temple would be reduced to rubble (Matthew 24:1-2, Luke 21:5-6), an unthinkable occurrence for the Jews of that day. Religious leaders would have ridiculed the idea that their massive temple could be razed. Yet in A.D. 70, the temple was indeed destroyed.

Additionally Isaiah 11:11-12, which was written more than 700 years before Christ, predicted that the Jews would one day return to Israel, after having been dispersed to points all around the world. At one time, skeptics pointed to this prediction (and a similar one in Ezekiel 37:21) as a prophecy that had never come to pass. Yet since the rebirth of the Jewish nation in 1948, Jewish individuals have, indeed, returned to Israel "from the four quarters of the earth" (Isaiah 11:12).

## Mistakes in the Bible?

Okay, I just have to say it. *Not everything in the Bible is true.*

For instance, Genesis 3:4 records that the Serpent told Adam and Eve there would be no penalty if they disobeyed God. That statement was not true.

But what you really want to know is if there are inconsistencies, false data, contradictions, or historical inaccuracies in the Bible. The answer is really no and yes. There are what scholars call "problem texts." For example, in Matthew 1:16 Joseph's father is listed as Jacob, and in Luke 3:23 Joseph is called the son of Heli. To clear up that question, you need to understand the way genealogies were used in ancient times. Often entire generations were skipped, or a person had two different names. The term "son" could mean son, grandson, or even great-great-great grandson.

Another type of problem text is exemplified in Deuteronomy

14:18 where a bat is named in a list of birds. Before we had scientific classification of animals based on whether or not they were warm- or cold-blooded, a bat was considered a bird because it could fly. The word *mammal* didn't even exist thousands of years ago. To understand the Bible the reader must take into consideration the time and culture of the original audience.

So are there difficult texts, problem passages which require some digging and extra study? Definitely. But are there contradictions and verified errors in God's Word? Definitely not. A good study Bible or commentary can help you clear up the questions surrounding many of the problem texts critics use to discredit the Bible. I've studied them and can assure you that there are no "problems" with your Bible or with the six historic core truths examined in this book. The Bible is the only reliable, accurate record of the account of God and His plan of salvation for the world.

---

### What the Bible Will Do for the Believer

- Convert the soul (John 20:31, James 1:18)
- Give guidance (Psalm 119:133)
- Produce joy (Psalm 119:14)
- Provide strength (1 John 2:14, Psalm 119:28)
- Instill hope (Psalm 119:74, 81)
- Produce growth (Acts 20:32, John 15)
- Convict of sin (Hebrews 4:12)
- Cleanse the conscience (John 15:3)
- Give comfort (Psalm 119:50) . . . and more!

## Why Inspiration Matters

If the Bible is God's Word and what it says was true when it was written, it is still true today and will be true tomorrow and forever. In the most crucial issues of life—I'm talking about subjects like God, human nature, right and wrong, sin, forgiveness, death, and eternity—you can't afford to guess what is true. Your life, now and in eternity, depends on whether or not what you believe is, in fact, true.

Here's an analysis of the Bible I think sums things up well:

The Bible contains the mind of God, the condition of man, the way of salvation, the doom of sinners, the happiness of believers. Its doctrines are holy, its precepts are binding, its histories are true, and its decisions unchangeable. Read the Bible to be wise and to be safe. Practice it to be holy. The Bible contains light to direct you, food to support you, and comfort to cheer you. It is the traveler's map, the pilgrim's staff, the pilot's compass, the soldier's sword, and the Christian's charter. Christ is its subject, our good its design, and the glory of God its end. The Bible should fill the memory, rule the heart, and guide the feet. Read it slowly, frequently, prayerfully. It is given to you in life, it will be open in the judgment, and be remembered forever. It involves the highest responsibility, rewards the greatest labor, and condemns all who trifle with its holy precepts.[9]

The origin, accuracy, and relevancy of the Bible are important to each of us. Fortunately, the evidence strongly indicates that the Bible is indeed God's Word, preserved for us to read, understand, and follow. Nearly 500 years ago, the great reformer Martin Luther gave us his take on God's Word:

> In the Bible God speaks. The Scriptures are His word.
> To hear or read the Scriptures is nothing else than to hear God Himself.[10]

You could spend your entire life, as some scholars have, researching the evidence in support of the Bible's accuracy. However, as Luther said, if you want to hear the voice of God, open your Bible. Read the Bible with an open mind and draw your own conclusions. A good, easy-to-understand starting point is the Gospel of John in the New Testament.

The words of Psalm 119:18 are a valid request that you may want to pray as you begin to study the Bible seriously:

> Open my eyes that I may see wonderful things in your law.

# Core Truth 2: Virgin Birth

## Christians Believe Jesus Was Born to a Virgin Named Mary

*If you, O LORD, kept a record of sins,*
*O LORD, who could* **stand**?

—PSALM 130:3

On "Truth Talk Live" radio a few years ago, I had a debate with an atheist I'll call Dr. R. I was in the studio, and he called in from his home phone. We began by debating the origin of the universe. I presented the argument that there had to be a cause or causer for the universe to exist.

Midway through the debate, he suddenly switched topics and began to talk about the problem of evil. I pointed out that if God (and an absolute standard of right, good, justice, perfection) does *not* exist, it makes no sense to fault the world for not measuring up to this nonexistent standard. In other words, if God does not exist, appealing to the "problem of evil" for God's nonexistence simply is not reasonable.

Finally, in the last five minutes of the radio broadcast, Dr. R said, "I'll tell you my number-one gripe with Christianity."

He explained that in the late 1950s he idolized the "minister to students" at his church. His youth pastor "morally defaulted"—left his wife and ran off with another woman. "I was crestfallen," said Dr. R. "If that kind of behavior is what Christianity is all about, I don't want anything to do with it. . . . So I have chosen to be an atheist."

"Its not about science at all," I said. "Dr. R, you got burned by a Christian who wasn't very Christlike. I am sorry that your youth pastor ran off with a woman who wasn't his wife, and I am sorry that that destroyed your faith in God. But we are not called to have our eyes on Christians, who may let us down; we are called to have our eyes on Christ, who will never let us down."

After the radio show was over, the sound engineer behind the glass held up the studio phone and motioned to me. "Dr. R wants to talk with you, off-air," he said.

The man on the other end said, "May I ask you something? You are a minister, a clergyman, right?"

I said, "Yes, I am an ordained minister. But I'm really just a saved sinner who loves Jesus and loves people."

There was a pause, and Dr. R said, "Would you pray for my wife? She has cancer."

Dr. R didn't need the perfect science proof. He needed a perfect Savior.

## The Virgin Birth Was Predicted in the Bible

Out of the billions and billions of humans who have lived on this planet, only one was born "perfect," without spiritual fault or sin. Jesus is that one, perfect human. That belief is a core truth of Christianity and is found throughout the Bible. Jesus' birth was the first sign that He was set apart from the rest of humanity—His birth was a complete miracle, a supernatural event.

Our key Bible reference in the New Testament is actually a quotation from Isaiah in the Old Testament:

> All this took place to fulfill what the Lord had said through
> the prophet: "The virgin will be with child and will give
> birth to a son, and they will call him Immanuel"—which
> means, "God with us." (Matthew 1:22-23)

When you read **virgin birth**, you probably think about Christmas and perhaps the Christmas carol "Silent Night":

> Silent night, holy night
> All is calm all is bright
> 'Round yon virgin Mother and Child
> Holy Infant so tender and mild
> Sleep in heavenly peace
> Sleep in heavenly peace[1]

It's great that Jesus' birth gets attention once a year, but after Christmas you may not hear another mention of the **virgin birth** until December rolls around again. The supernatural way that Jesus was born is a core truth of Christianity that deserves our focus more than once a year. The Bible tells us that Jesus' mother was not physically impregnated by a human father. Mary carried and delivered the baby Jesus, and the godly man Joseph helped raise Him. But Scripture is clear that Joseph and Mary did not conceive Jesus.

God is the Father of Jesus.

Let's read a familiar part of the Christmas story—the angel Gabriel's announcement to Mary that she would have a child:

> The angel went to her and said, "Greetings, you who are highly favored! The Lord is with you."
>
> Mary was greatly troubled at his words and wondered what kind of greeting this might be. But the angel said to her, "Do not be afraid, Mary, you have found favor with God. You will be with child and give birth to a son, and you are to give him the name Jesus. He will be great and will be called the Son of the Most High. The Lord God will give him the throne of his father David, and he will reign over the house of Jacob forever; his kingdom will never end."
>
> "How will this be," Mary asked the angel, "since I am a virgin?"
>
> The angel answered, "The Holy Spirit will come upon you, and the power of the Most High will over-shadow you. So the holy one to be born will be called the Son of God." (Luke 1:28-35)

## Why the Virgin Birth Matters

Can a modern, educated person really believe that Mary was a virgin, as the Bible says? Can you really believe in the miracle of

Jesus' birth? There are plenty of skeptics who say no. These people include journalists, historians, and even some ministers. They go further and say it doesn't really matter how Jesus came into the world.

But they are wrong.

An unshakable faith rests on the Bible's truthfulness about the **virgin birth** of Jesus Christ. The **virgin birth** is central to establishing that Jesus is God. It's central to understanding what He did when He died on the cross for our sins. It's central to understanding how He rose from the grave and later was caught up to heaven in the clouds (see Acts 1). Everything that is supernatural about Jesus is dependent upon His supernatural entry into this world.

Yes, Jesus arrived just like every other human baby, after the normal development in His mother's womb. But to carry out God's plan for forgiveness and salvation, Jesus came into the world in a way unlike any other baby—ever: He did not have a human father.

Several Bible passages point to the **virgin birth** directly, and others support the claim indirectly. Very early in the Bible, after Adam and Eve sinned, God promised a Savior who would one day destroy the work of Satan. The **virgin birth** is implied in Genesis 3:15, when God says to the serpent (Satan):

> "And I will put enmity between you and the woman, and
> between your seed and her seed; he shall bruise you on
> the head, and you shall bruise him on the heel." (NASB)

"Her seed," or Eve's offspring, is an unusual reference to children. Normally in ancient times, children were called "the seed of the man." But Jesus was not the product of a human father. He was "the seed of the woman."

Another familiar Old Testament promise was given in Isaiah 7:14, which Matthew quotes in our key reference. Isaiah wrote this promise more than 700 years before Jesus was born: "Therefore the Lord himself will give you a sign: The virgin will be with child and will give birth to a son, and will call him Immanuel."

## Sin—Your Unavoidable Inheritance

When people talk about the "**virgin birth**," what they actually mean is the virgin conception. Jesus' supernatural conception is the miracle of spiritual and biological necessity.

While Christ had to come in the flesh, He could not come in a body of sinful flesh if He was to be "in the likeness of sinful man to be a sin offering" (Romans 8:3). You see, in the Old Testament, the Jewish people brought perfect animals—the best they had—to be sacrificed for sin. Likewise, in order to be the perfect sacrifice to wash away the sins of humanity, the Savior, brought for sacrifice, had to be free of any defect.

So why a virgin conception? Well, it's because of what we've inherited from our first father, Adam.

We've all dreamed about having a rich uncle who surprises the family by leaving a fortune in cash. "I've never inherited anything," someone told me once.

I replied, "You may not have a wealthy relative to put you in his will, but there is something that has definitely been passed on to you."

"Oh yeah?" the person asked. "When would that have been?"

I explained what the Bible says about our unavoidable family legacy. "The day you were born, you had an inheritance. Adam's sin-guilt was passed on to you the day you came into the world."

The Bible says that sin and death came into the human race through our ancestor, Adam (see 1 Corinthians 15:21-22). You could say we're sinners in two ways: by birth and by choice. We have sinful tendencies, and we commit sinful actions.

If Jesus had a human father, he would also have inherited Adam's sin-guilt. He would not have been the perfect sacrifice, the "lamb without blemish" (1 Peter 1:19). He would not have been qualified to die in our place. His supernatural birth as the "seed of the woman," born of a virgin, made possible His perfect sacrifice for the sins of the world.

## Common Objections to Belief in the Virgin Birth

The first objection some scholars raise centers on the language of the Bible. Some translations of Isaiah 7:14 read "a young woman shall conceive and bear a son" rather than "a virgin shall conceive." When Isaiah was written in the Hebrew language—the original language of the Old Testament—did the word that's translated "virgin" mean what we think it means? Had Mary really never had sexual intercourse with a man, or was she just "a young woman"?

The Isaiah 7 word that is usually translated "virgin" is the Hebrew word *almah*. It occurs only seven times in the entire Bible. Scholars have noted that in every case, "virgin" is the only meaning attached to the word.[2]

About 200 years before the birth of Jesus, the Old Testament was translated from Hebrew into Greek. (Greek was the common language of the known world at the time, and this was to make the Scriptures easier for the people of that time to read and understand.) When the translators came to this passage in Isaiah 7:14, they rendered the Hebrew word *almah* as the Greek word *parthenos*, which can only mean "virgin." Now keep in mind that this translation took place two centuries before Jesus was born. The translators trusted what the prophet Isaiah had written. Though they may not have fully understood what the verse meant, they upheld the miraculous prediction of the **virgin birth**.

### *Do Miracles Happen?*
The second objection to the **virgin birth** centers on disbelief in miracles. For about 150 years, ever since the theory of evolution became popular, there has been a widespread belief that miracles do not occur. Naturalism became the accepted point of view for

---

**Four Ways God Has Made Human Bodies**

1. God once made a human body apart from any male/female reproductive activity. He made Adam from the dust of the ground.
2. God once made a human body from a man. He made Eve from one of Adam's ribs.
3. God makes a human body through the natural sexual activity of both a man and a woman.
4. And in a onetime, never-to-be-repeated event, God made a human body through a woman alone. Jesus was conceived by the Holy Spirit in the womb of Mary, a virgin.

many people who live in Europe and North America. Naturalists believe that nature—the material, physical world and energy—is all there is. Naturalists think that scientific laws can account for all phenomena on our planet and in our solar system, our galaxy, and countless galaxies beyond. Naturalism says there can be no miracles, absolutely nothing supernatural. For the naturalist, God is not a factor in either the creation of the world or the ongoing operation of the world. Naturalism says that God does not exist since existence can't be proven. The universe evolved, they believe, and things just continue on, following the course of nature. One of the objections people raise against the **virgin birth** is that such a thing would be "against nature."

"The virgin birth story arose at a time when people were too ignorant to know better," I have heard skeptics say. "We all know how babies are made."

Think of the arrogance behind that statement. Do they think that people 2,700 years ago also didn't know how babies are made? But in a naturalistic worldview, there is no room for the miraculous, so they have to resort to ridiculous charges to maintain their point of view. As C. S. Lewis wrote:

> He [Joseph, Mary's husband] knew just as well as any
> modern gynecologist that in the ordinary course of nature,
> women do not have babies, unless they have lain with
> men. The thing is impossible unless the regular processes
> of nature were, in this particular case, being over-ruled or
> supplemented by something from beyond nature.[3]

How does all of this relate to the **virgin birth** of Jesus Christ? Simple. If God is powerful enough to create this planet and all of the people on it, as the Bible says, then why wouldn't He have the ability to work within this world He made? If God could make males and females, set into motion the process of human reproduction, couldn't He cause a mother to give birth apart from a biological father? Of course, God could do that. And the Bible says that He did.

Naturalism says that the world must operate only by scientific laws that can be observed, measured, and sometimes controlled. A major objection to the **virgin birth** is that it is not natural.

The Christian response to this objection is based on a complex Greek word: Duh! The fact that **virgin births** do not happen naturally is not a news flash. A **virgin birth** is a miracle, an act of God. That's why Isaiah 7 said that it would be a "sign" to Israel.

Without the **virgin birth**, Jesus would not have been the unique Son of God but merely another first-century rabbi. Eliminate the **virgin birth** from Jesus' unique characteristics, and His deeds and ministry are not as significant. Who He was, what He did, what He said—all of these lose their unique character and binding authority if Jesus was a mortal like us.

## The Greatest Act of Caring

Jesus told His disciples a parable about a shepherd who rescued one of his lost lambs, even though it meant risking his own life (Matthew 18:12-14). To go after the wandering sheep involved a high degree of commitment, but the faithful shepherd was willing to do it.

In reality, the lost sheep represents all of humanity. Our only hope of safe return to the flock is through Jesus, the greatest shepherd of all.

You matter to God. Jesus' **virgin birth**, sinless life, miraculous deeds, and death and resurrection on our behalf are proof positive—He loves you. The most significant event of all time was God's entrance into human history. As many have pointed out, history really is "His story," and the **virgin birth** is an integral part of that story.

It has always interested me that all of the attempts to bypass the **virgin birth** smuggle in a subtle elevation of man. Many have no problem making Jesus to be less than what the Bible says. At the same time, they will make man out to be more than what the Bible teaches. "Man is basically good," people reason. Many simply do not believe that God would do anything so drastic as to literally enter history through a virgin's womb and exit through a virgin tomb.

Because of sin, there was need for a Savior. Jesus Christ met all of the qualifications for "saviorhood." Psalm 40, written hundreds of years before Jesus was born and later cited in Hebrews 10:5 as proof of Jesus' authenticity, predicts that God would one day take on human form:

"Sacrifice and offering you did not desire, but a body you prepared for me."

In explaining that Christ's death was the full and complete "sacrifice" and "offering" for sin, Hebrews 10:5 repeats this Old Testament prophecy. Trying to understand this even in a small way stretches our mind . . . but God did prepare a body for Himself to inhabit.

### "I Believe the Bible; I Just Don't Read It"

Every year around Christmas, you'll find articles in magazines that question the events surrounding the birth of Jesus. In December 2004, a *Newsweek* article quoted scholars who said the **virgin birth** was more myth than reality, more fiction than historical fact. But surprisingly, the same magazine published a poll that found 79 percent of American adults say they believe in the **virgin birth**.[4] That's encouraging! Despite decades of false theories and skeptical objections, most people still trust the Bible.

Unfortunately, other surveys show they don't read it! Even most Christians neglect to read the Bible and, as a result, miss out on the core truths at the foundation of our faith.

After hearing me speak on the **virgin birth** at his church, a teen came up to me to say thanks. "I mean, wow, I never knew this! This seems really important." He got it . . . and I pray that you get it, too, and are ready to move on to the next core truth.

# Core Truth 3: Deity of Christ

## Christians Believe Jesus Christ Is God

> *"I am not alone. I **stand** with*
> *the Father, who sent me."*
> —JOHN 8:16

You can toss the greatest of compliments to Jesus Christ and never get an argument from me. He was the greatest among men, the wisest of all teachers, the most loving and kind human ever born. A gentle shepherd. A compassionate friend. A courageous prophet.

One teen told me, "My history teacher said that Jesus was a martyr, dying for His faith, and that there have been many martyrs throughout history. It's ironic that people chose to make such a big deal about Jesus, since other martyrs were equally sincere."

Oh, yes, did I mention that Jesus was sincere—and true to Himself? That's got to be the highest compliment of all in today's world. He stood up for what He believed in. More than that, He was willing to lay His life down for it, too.

Hardly anyone has a problem calling Jesus "good," but many draw the line at calling Jesus "God."

When scholars speak of the **deity** of Christ, they are referring to the Christian belief that Jesus is actually God. The word **deity** (*DEE-uh-tee*) is from the Latin word for God. The Bible teaches that Jesus is fully God.

Many people throughout history have claimed to represent God. Jesus, however, claimed to *be* God. Some religious leaders have spoken *for* the Lord; Jesus spoke *as* the Lord. The world has seen the birth of many individuals who turned out to be *godly*. But only one person who came into the world was *God*.

Verses throughout the Old Testament describe many unique details of the promised Savior. In the New Testament we see all of those characteristics wrapped up in one person: Jesus Christ.

Isaiah 9:6 is a key reference written more than 700 years before Jesus was born:

> For to us a child is born, to us a son is given, and the government will be on his shoulders. And he will be called Wonderful Counselor, Mighty God, Everlasting Father, Prince of Peace.

This Old Testament passage is quoted in the New Testament book of Matthew, as an angel tells Joseph about the special baby that his fiancée would soon deliver:

"She will give birth to a son, and you are to give him the name Jesus, because he will save his people from their sins." All this took place to fulfill what the Lord had said through the prophet: "The virgin will be with child and will give birth to a son, and they will call him Immanuel"—which means, "God with us." (1:21-23)

## A King Like No Other

Years later, as Jesus stood before Pilate, the Roman governor who would unjustly sentence Him to death, He was questioned about His identity. Pilate had met kings and leaders and was also a man of some power. He found it strange that any true king would end up arrested. Pilate apparently had a hard time understanding why Jesus would allow Himself to be taken into custody. *What type of king are you?* Pilate may have wondered. Their conversation is recorded in John 18:

> "What is it you have done?" [Pilate asked.]
> Jesus said, "My kingdom is not of this world. If it were, my servants would fight to prevent my arrest by the Jews. But now my kingdom is from another place."
> "You are a king, then!" said Pilate.
> Jesus answered, "You are right in saying I am a king. In fact, for this reason I was born, and for this I came into the world, to testify to the truth. Everyone on the side of truth listens to me." (verses 35-37)

Jesus has given clear responses to Pilate's questions. He answers that yes, He is a king. But then Jesus makes two more claims that seem to catch Pilate off guard: He was born for a specific purpose, and He planned His own entry into the world—"for this reason . . . I came into the world."

Hit the pause button and think about this. No other person in history could truthfully make that statement. You and I (and Pilate) were each born through the activity of a father and mother. Our mothers carried us for nine months, and we were eventually born. But face it—none of us really had any involvement in the matter.

What kind of man can say, "I intentionally planned and carried out my entry into this world"? Who could exist before he was born? There is only one logical answer—God.

But Jesus had said something else that caught Pilate's ear. I can see Jesus' eyes—piercing, yet inviting—as He told Pilate, "Everyone on the side of truth listens to me."

### Some of Jesus' Best-Known Miracles

Jesus' supernatural birth is only the beginning of the miracles. During His life here on earth, Jesus

- turned water into wine at a wedding
- fed 5,000 people plus
- raised Lazarus from the grave
- raised a widow's dead son
- healed a soldier's ear (Jesus' last miracle before the Cross)
- came back after being dead for three days
- ascended straight to heaven

Pilate certainly had been exposed to Greek philosophy, Roman scholars, and other ancient thinkers. He also probably knew a fair amount about the Jewish prophets who had predicted the coming of a great one, a deliverer, a messiah. But standing before him that day was a teacher different from anyone he had ever encountered. "Everyone on the side of truth listens to me."

Pilate had heard teachers give conflicting, vague opinions about life. Even the Jews, who had writings from God, couldn't always agree on what their Scriptures meant. Yet here was a man who claimed to have the truth. In fact, this man seemed to be saying that He was the key to truth.

Pilate responded as best he could: " 'What is truth?' he asked. With this he went out again to the Jews and said, 'I find no basis for a charge against him.' " (John 18:38).

## Jesus Is the Savior Foretold in Scripture

Jesus is unique among all the people who have ever lived. He is the "Son of God," yet "God the Son." Before Jesus was born, Mary and Joseph knew that the child they would raise was special, and His uniqueness became more and more clear as He grew up. When Jesus wound up missing on a trip from Jerusalem, Joseph and Mary discovered their 12-year-old three days later in the temple courts amazing the educated religious leaders with His knowledge (see Luke 2:41-50).

At age 30, Jesus read the Word of God before a group gathered in a synagogue. The people attending worship that day were in for a surprise!

He went to Nazareth, where he had been brought up, and on the Sabbath day he went into the synagogue, as was his custom. And he stood up to read. The scroll of the prophet Isaiah was handed to him. Unrolling it, he found the place where it is written:

"The Spirit of the Lord is on me, because he has anointed me to preach good news to the poor. He has sent me to proclaim freedom for the prisoners and recovery of sight for the blind, to release the oppressed, to proclaim the year of the Lord's favor."

Then he rolled up the scroll, gave it back to the attendant and sat down. The eyes of everyone in the synagogue were fastened on him, and he began by saying to them, "Today this scripture is fulfilled in your hearing." (Luke 4:16-21)

The people who heard Jesus read in the synagogue that day realized He did not pick out just any verse to read. They understood that He had specifically turned to a passage that dealt with the Savior who was to be sent. Think of the surprise and awe that fell on the crowd that day. They had heard priests teach on this passage before, but no one had ever claimed to be the person whom Scripture was speaking about.

Jesus was sending out the message that this beloved portion of God's Word was about Him.

## About Those First Four Books
## in Your New Testament

So how do we know these things about Jesus? It's all there in the first four books of the New Testament: Matthew, Mark, Luke, and John. The word *gospel* means "good news." Because the opening books of the New Testament so clearly present Jesus and His gift of salvation, the writers of these books are sometimes called the "four evangelists." In preserving the good news about Jesus' life, actions, and message, the writers do live up to the title.

Each of the New Testament Gospels has similarities to the others. All four are full of facts about Jesus and present Him as the Messiah whose life, death, and resurrection make it possible for sins to be forgiven. But each Gospel also has its own unique emphasis.

Matthew, which was probably written for Jewish readers, convincingly shows that Jesus is the promised Messiah. Matthew quotes verses from the Old Testament 53 times, more than any other Gospel.

Mark, which may have been written primarily for non-Jewish readers, shows Jesus to be humanity's most dedicated Servant. Jesus told His disciples, "Whoever wants to be first must be slave of all" (Mark 10:44). In laying down His life to save us, Jesus performed the ultimate act of service. Mark quotes from the Old Testament 36 times.

Luke includes many historical details and unique facts. William Ramsay, an expert on ancient history, initially became convinced of the Bible's accuracy through his study of the Gospel of Luke. He wrote:

> I take the view that Luke's history is unsurpassed in regard
> to its trustworthiness. . . . You may press the words of
> Luke in a degree beyond any other historian's, and they
> stand the keenest scrutiny and the hardest treatment.[1]

The attention to detail is understandable in light of the fact that Luke, the writer of both the Gospel of Luke and Acts, was a doctor—a man of science. The Gospel of Luke, which frequently describes Jesus as "the Son of Man," presents Him as the perfect man. Luke was writing with a Greek audience in mind, a culture that could appreciate the flawless human qualities of Jesus. He quotes from the Old Testament 25 times.

Matthew, Mark, and Luke all present clear evidence for the **deity** of Jesus, but it's the Gospel of John that focuses on Jesus' identity as God right from the very first verse: "In the beginning was the Word, and the Word was with God, and the Word was God" (John 1:1).

Who is "the Word" whom John identifies as God? Jesus Christ.

The Word became flesh and made his dwelling among
us. We have seen his glory, the glory of the One and
Only, who came from the Father, full of grace and truth.
(John 1:14)

John presents Jesus as God in flesh. As one of the closest disciples of Jesus, he wrote as an eyewitness—"We have seen his glory"—and he testifies that what he writes is true (John 21:24). John quotes from the Old Testament 20 times.

John is also the only Gospel writer to include the account of "doubting Thomas," an account that shows clearly that Jesus and His disciples all considered Him to be God.

After His resurrection, Jesus made several appearances to His followers to prove He was alive. On the evening of the day of Jesus' resurrection, His fearful disciples were gathered behind locked doors when Jesus "came and stood among them" (John

20:19). When He showed them His pierced hands, their fear turned to joy.

But one of the disciples, Thomas, was not with them for this joyful reunion with Jesus, and he made it clear it would take more than his friends' eyewitness account to prove that Jesus was alive:

> [Thomas said], "Unless I see the nail marks in his hands and put my finger where the nails were, and put my hand into his side, I will not believe it."
>
> A week later his disciples were in the house again, and Thomas was with them. Though the doors were locked, Jesus came and stood among them and said, "Peace be with you!" Then he said to Thomas, "Put your finger here; see my hands. Reach out your hand and put it into my side. Stop doubting and believe." (John 20:25-27)

What follows is one of the clearest declarations of the **deity** of Jesus Christ in the Bible: Thomas said to him, "My Lord and my God!" (John 20:28).

If Jesus was not truly God, He would not have allowed Thomas to say this, since it would have been blasphemy to call a mere man God. John wrote his Gospel to convince you and me of what Thomas at first would not believe:

> Jesus did many other miraculous signs in the presence of his disciples, which are not recorded in this book. But these are written that you may believe that Jesus is the Christ, the Son of God, and that by believing you may have life in his name. (John 20:30-31)

The number of lives touched by the Gospel of John cannot be measured this side of heaven. Even today, as the Scriptures are first translated into obscure languages that only a few people speak, the Gospel of John is often the first (and sometimes the only) biblical book to be completed. John 3:16—"For God so loved the world . . ."—is only one of many well-known and well-loved verses.

## Why Deity Matters

After finishing his sophomore term in college, Brett took a year off to do relief work with a humanitarian agency. While helping to build dwellings and shelters in Africa, Brett was approached by a religious group. "At first," he said, "I was just glad to talk with some other Americans and to make friends. They talked about the Bible and used a lot of the same words I had heard in church."

But the teachings of this religious organization contradicted what Brett had heard all of his life in church. In forceful and convincing ways, members of the group told Brett that Jesus was *not* the Son of God and that only those who accepted the group's unique perspective on Scripture would go to heaven. Far from home, doubting and confused, Brett felt a growing sense of desperation.

"They were really messing with my mind," Brett said. "They said I was going to burn in hell if I did not accept their teachings. The pressure they put on me was almost unbearable."

One day it occurred to Brett that the group spent most of their time attacking what Christians believe about Jesus. Over and over the group told Brett that Jesus was not the Son of God but only a created "angel."

"I was kicking myself inside for not having listened better in Sunday school!" Brett remembers. "There was only one Bible verse that I could halfway recall from memory. That was John 3:16: 'For God so loved the world that he gave his one and only Son, that whoever believes in him shall not perish but have eternal life.'"

Brett reasoned that in order to die for the sins of the world, Jesus *had* to have been God in the flesh—**deity**—not some created being. "I suddenly realized how important the things they teach at church are. When I remembered that Jesus is God in human form—the actual Lord who came to earth from heaven—only then was I able to hold my own against the distortions of this cult."

Brett came back with a deeper understanding of the importance of *doctrine*. In this case, knowledge of the doctrine of Christ's **deity** helped Brett to withstand the pressure of a group whose beliefs (and behavior) were unbiblical.

Many religions talk about Jesus, sometimes in words that sound pretty good. Muslims say that He was a prophet from God, but they deny He is God or that He died on the cross. Hinduism says that Jesus was a great teacher. Other Eastern religions, such as Buddhism, teach that Jesus was mystical and wise. Wicca and various forms of paganism may say that Jesus was only a man, or even that He never actually lived.

The Mormons say that Jesus was "an elder brother" who became a god, and the Jehovah's Witnesses teach that Jesus was not God, but an angel that God created.

In Matthew 16:15-16 Jesus asked His disciples, "Who do you say I am?" Peter answered him, "You are the Christ, the Son of the living God."

*Who do **you** say Jesus is?*

## More Thoughts on Deity

C. S. Lewis said that if Jesus wasn't who He claimed to be, then He is really of no importance. However, if Jesus is the Son of God and Savior as He claimed, then He is of infinite importance. The one thing that Jesus can't be, Lewis observed, is just someone of moderate importance.[2]

In other words, because Jesus is indeed the God-man, the risen Savior, the ever-present Friend, the soon-to-return King, and the final Judge or Rewarder of all people—because Jesus Christ is the Lord—believers should follow and honor Him in every area of life.

Thomas Watson, a Christian leader in England three centuries ago, reflected on how everything about Jesus seemed to be just right: "No one has yet discovered the word Jesus ought to have said, none suggested the better word He might have said. . . . This man alone never made a false step."[3]

The English writer G. K. Chesterton wrestled intellectually with writers and thinkers who readily acknowledged Jesus was "good" but not "God." Chesterton had struggled to understand why so many of his peers could not seem to get a handle on Jesus. Jesus did many things that only God could do, such as forgive sins. He lived a life of perfection—better in every way than any other person. Who could this be, who seemed so godlike, yet perfectly human?

In his book *Orthodoxy*, Chesterton shared an insight that occurred to him one day "like a thunderbolt." Though the language is nearly 100 years old, you can sense that he had an "Aha!" moment:

> Suppose we heard an unknown man spoken of by many
> men. Suppose we were puzzled to hear that some men
> said he was too tall, and some too short; some objected
> to his fatness, some lamented his leanness; some thought
> him too dark, and some too fair. One explanation (as has
> been already admitted) would be that he might be an odd
> shape. But there is another explanation. He might be the
> right shape. . . . Perhaps, after all, it is Christianity that is
> sane, and all its critics that are "mad" in various ways.[4]

Chesterton was saying that the problem is with humans, not with Jesus. Jesus is the Perfect One. We humans are the ones who get it wrong all too often.

For the person who comes with an honest heart and open mind, the facts about Jesus are there to be examined. Is Jesus God? Why couldn't He be God? Why couldn't God walk the dirt of planet Earth if He chose?

Why couldn't God speak to His prophets, enter the womb of a virgin, live among His creatures, and die for their souls if He wanted to?

The answer is, "He could." And the Bible (along with lots of compelling evidence) tells us, "He did."

# FIVE

# Core Truth 4: Atonement

## Christians Believe Jesus Paid for Their Sins

*O LORD, God of Israel, you are righteous! . . .*
*Here we are before you in our guilt, though because*
*of it not one of us can* **stand** *in your presence.*

—EZRA 9:15

Jesus died for the sins of the world.

Do you believe that? I mean do you *really* believe that? Jesus died for the sins of the world—the *whole* world! That has to be about the most powerful, awe-inspiring statement that a human could ponder. A banner at an evangelistic event put it this way: "Christ for the World"—one man giving Himself for all people.

The core truths of Christianity have many skeptics. Want to know what I've discovered about the people who have trouble believing that Jesus died for the sins of the world? Many of them are Christians.

I was speaking to a group of Christian teens about Jesus paying our sin debt on the cross when one of them asked, "Alex, does everybody get a chance to be saved?"

"Jesus offers salvation to everyone," I said, "though not all accept it."

"But what about the really, really bad people?"

"Jesus fully paid for our sins," I replied. "Do you all understand that every person in this room can ask for forgiveness . . . and really be forgiven?"

"Yes!" everyone said in unison.

"Could a bank robber even get forgiveness?"

"Yes!"

"Could Jesus even forgive a murderer?"

"Yes!"

"Could Osama bin Laden be saved?"

"No!"

Well, what does the Bible say? Can the grace of God extend to Osama bin Laden?

## Jesus Paid the Penalty for the Sins of the World

Our discovery of Christianity's core truths can't climb any higher than the **atonement**, a biblical word that means "to make payment for a debt." In a number of places, the Bible presents (and explains) the news that Jesus paid for our sins with His own blood. I am glad that the Bible covers this subject in great detail. God knew that our human brains would struggle to understand this amazing truth.

Here is a key reference in the New Testament: "[Jesus] is the atoning sacrifice for our sins, and not only for ours but also for the sins of the whole world" (1 John 2:2).

Jesus' death and resurrection provided a complete and full payment for human sin—my sin, your sin, everyone's sin.

## Enough Forgiveness to Go Around

*Crowded.* That's the main word I can think of to describe airports. Traveling to speaking engagements over the years, I've learned to set aside extra time for possible delays. Likely delays. Okay, I plan for almost certain delays.

A really busy airport area is Terminal B at Bush Intercontinental Airport in Houston, Texas. Every time I go there, the building is full of people. Regardless of where all of these travelers may be headed, the one common characteristic is that they all want to hurry up and get there, even if they don't have a ticket. This phenomenon has resulted in the creation of a whole new race of human beings. They are called "standbys." Airlines sell tickets to standbys even when the plane is full. Standbys hope that some people won't show up.

Recently in Terminal B at the airport in Houston, I overheard a conversation between an airline official and some standbys. It was late at night, the flight was behind schedule, and the standby list was long. There must have been 15 standbys staring at information screens and whispering.

Suddenly two of them heard their names called. "Yessss!" the male hissed to his female companion. This is standby speak that means, "I'm so glad we'll not be spending the night in this airport."

But as the couple was about to walk down the corridor to get on the plane, a ticket agent stopped them. Another airline agent walked up, escorting a different couple who also clutched standby tickets.

I observed the happiness of the first couple evaporate immediately. Apparently, the other standby couple exercised some kind of priority power—maybe a billion frequent-flyer points. Is there a secret power structure among the standby people?

"Space is limited, and the airplane has only two seats left," I heard the ticket agent gently say. "If I let these two people on, that means both of you will have to stay behind. I'm sorry."

## No Standbys for Heaven

The **atonement** doesn't work like the standby list at airports. A trip to heaven is offered to every one of the billions of humans who have ever lived. Consider what John the Baptist declared about Jesus: "Look, the Lamb of God, who takes away the sin of the world!" (John 1:29).

I'm glad the Bible doesn't say that Jesus takes away some of the sins of some of the people. No. The Bible promises that Jesus would take care of the sin problem—completely. Some receive God's gift, and others reject it. But heaven—and God's way to get there—can accommodate everyone.

Back in my home state of North Carolina, a city auction to raise money for charity included items for sale that had been donated as well as items that had been lost and found or recovered by city authorities.

My wife and I watched a young boy run toward a row of bicycles. "There's my bike!" he exclaimed. "That's it!"

I guess the boy had somehow lost his bike and came with his

dad to the auction to buy another one. As the boy began to wheel his bike away, I could hear his father explain he couldn't do that.

The boy looked confused. "But it's my bike," he said. "It belongs to me."

His father showed him the inventory tag tied to the handlebars. When the auction started, they would bid and try to buy the bicycle back. "Son, you will have had that bike twice," he said. "You owned it, and you will have bought it back."

That's like our relationship to God. The Bible says that God owns everything in the world because He created the world. Psalm 100:3 says, "Know that the LORD is God. It is he who made us, and we are his." God owns us, every one of us, but like a beloved possession that got lost, the human race rebelled and became separated from Him. We became lost.

But Jesus has bought us back. Each follower of Jesus Christ has a special relationship with Him. We know that a person's sins are forgiven when he turns to Christ, and the Bible promises that his name is written in heaven (see Luke 10:20, Hebrews 12:23, Revelation 21:27). But each Christian can reflect on the knowledge that God both created him and, through the cross of Jesus Christ, bought him. God loved each of us so much that He was willing to own us twice.

## Basic Facts About the Atonement

**Atonement** means "to make payment for a debt." In a court of law, for example, a judge might order you to "make restitution" to someone you have wronged. The concept of **atonement** applies to situations that involve paying for an offense.

Most people understand the need to take responsibility for

their own debts. But would you be willing to pay off the debts of a stranger? How would you feel about covering the bills owed by someone who never showed appreciation, who maybe even hated you? I know what you're thinking: "Forget it! If someone can't pay me back or at least say 'Thank you,' he's on his own!"

Fortunately for us, that's not how God responded to our sin debt. God has a really big heart. Jesus was deeply and emotionally stirred when He looked out at the masses of helpless people, "like sheep without a shepherd" (Matthew 9:36). Because of His great love, God was willing to give His Son as the payment for our sins (John 3:16, Romans 5:8).

### Atonement Is Needed Because of the High Cost of Sin

"He paid a debt He didn't owe, because I owed a debt I couldn't pay."

Those words from an old gospel song sound like a tongue-twister, but they're true. The Bible says that Jesus "reconciled" man with God:

> For if, when we were God's enemies, we were reconciled
> to him through the death of his Son, how much more,
> having been reconciled, shall we be saved through his life!
> Not only is this so, but we also rejoice in God through
> our Lord Jesus Christ, through whom we have now
> received reconciliation. (Romans 5:10-11)

In other words, Jesus makes it possible for sinful and rebellious humans to have a right relationship with God, who is holy, perfect, pure, and sinless. Did Jesus have any guilt or sins of His own to deal with? No. On a mountain-sized altar outside of

Jerusalem, Jesus willingly died on a cross as a perfect sacrifice for our sins. Our sin debt is paid for and forgiven.

### *Atonement and Redemption: God's "To Do" List*

At the heart of the gospel, the Bible's good news, are the concepts of **atonement** and redemption. As stated, the doctrine of **atonement** means that Jesus paid for our sins. Redemption means we're delivered, set free, through payment of a price. Those of us whose sins have been paid are "redeemed"—set free from sin.

In ancient times, prisoners of war could be released by payment of a ransom. The Bible says that Christ came to "give his life as a ransom for many" (Mark 10:45). The Bible promises that believers have "redemption through his blood" (Ephesians 1:7).

All of God's activities could be listed under two categories:

God's great work of creation.
God's great work of redemption.

In fact, the Bible could be summarized as "God's plan of redemption through Jesus Christ."

So why are some people not saved? Redemption involves the Savior and the saved. The main characters in the great story of redemption are the Person who is Christ and the people who need Christ. Redemption from sin is *required* of all, and redemption from sin is *offered* to all, but redemption from sin is not *received* by all. Sadly, some individuals reject God's love and His free offer of redemption from sin.

The Christian concept of redemption is unique among the world's religions. Maybe you've heard someone say, "All religions basically teach the same things." This is a popular assumption, but it is incorrect. Some religions teach that people should offer things to try to earn God's favor. The Bible teaches that there's nothing you can do to earn God's favor. Salvation is a gift from God.

It takes only simple faith, or trust, to receive Jesus into your life. As you do that, several wonderful things take place. The redemption that believers have in Christ includes:

1. Forgiveness of all sin and guilt, past, present, and future
2. Being declared righteous, or just, in God's sight
3. Adoption into God's family

The Bible used legal terminology familiar to its readers when it was written. Jesus has freed those captive to sin, just like slaves or political prisoners who had been set free. Our release was made possible through the payment of a price—Jesus' blood. Though we were not naturally related to God (our sin separated us from the Lord), we were given the status of being full members of God's family.

## Why Atonement Matters

**Atonement** gets to the crux of the matter. The word *crucial* is from the Latin word *crux*, which means "the central point," or "cross." Jesus' work on the cross is the real crux of the Christian message. On the cross, redemption's price was paid by God Himself:

> For you know that it was not with perishable things such
> as silver or gold that you were redeemed from the empty

way of life handed down to you from your forefathers, but with the precious blood of Christ, a lamb without blemish or defect. (1 Peter 1:18-19)

The Old Testament talked about what the promised Savior would one day accomplish. Isaiah 53:5 says that He would be "pierced for our transgressions" (our sins). Without doubt, Scripture presents human redemption as completely dependent on the blood of Christ. Revelation 1:5 says that the blood of Christ "has freed us from our sins."

Hebrews 9 teaches that Christ's work on the cross was God's once-and-for-all payment of the sin debt. In fact, without Christ's blood payment, redemption would be impossible (verse 22). (See also Isaiah 55:1-7, John 3:16, John 6:37, John 11:26, Acts 10:43, Romans 10:13, Revelation 22:17.)

Some of Jesus' last words on the cross were "It is finished." These were not words of defeat, but of victory! Nothing more had to be done—or could have been done. In dying, Jesus made it possible for lost people to live.

## How This Relates to My Life

Have you seen the bumper sticker that reads: 3 nails + 1 cross = 4given? It's short and to the point, and it's accurate.

When we really think about what Jesus endured to pay for our sins, it is humbling. He suffered the nails and wounds of the cross and accepted the fury of God's judgment to be poured on Himself. It is no wonder that planet Earth shook and daylight fled (see Matthew 27). All of the darkness, pain, and death that human evil would ever produce was being put on heaven's loving King, Jesus.

A middle-school student who still felt bad about something he had done, even though he had asked for forgiveness, sent me an e-mail: "It's hard to think that God still loves me."

In my response, I explained that Jesus made it possible for us to become Christians and also to grow and mature in our faith. Because of Christ's **atonement**, we are still His even when we blow it and sin: "If we confess our sins, he is faithful and just and will forgive us our sins and purify us from all unrighteousness" (1 John 1:9).

In the life of every Christian, awareness of the **atonement** should breed a sincere appreciation for all that Jesus did. A consistent walk and witness demonstrate thanks for the gift believers have been given. We should be willing to share the truth of Jesus with those around us who may be trusting in the wrong thing for salvation.

---

### We Belong to God in Several Ways

1. He created us: "It is he who made us, and we are his" (Psalm 100:3)
2. He saved us: "You are not your own; you were bought at a price" (1 Corinthians 6:19-20)
3. He justified us: God will declare us righteous if we believe in Him who raised Jesus from the dead (see Romans 4:24 and 5:1)
4. He sealed us: "You were marked in him with a seal, the promised Holy Spirit" (Ephesians 1:13)

## Even Osama bin Laden Can Be Saved

You can't stretch the truth too far when it comes to saving the lost. That's what I told the group of students who thought Osama bin Laden was too far gone even for God to redeem.

"Now wait a minute!" I told them. "Doesn't the Bible say, 'Everyone who calls on the name of the Lord will be saved'?"[2] Didn't Jesus promise in John 6:37 that 'whoever comes to me I will never drive away,' or reject?"

"Wow! I never thought about it that way," someone said. "Jesus could really save anybody."

# Core Truth 5: Resurrection

## Christians Believe Jesus Christ Rose from the Dead

> *I know that my Redeemer lives, and that*
> *in the end he will **stand** upon the earth.*
> —JOB 19:25

Have you ever seen a 1957 Chevrolet Bel Air? That's one hot car. Even back when I was a kid, the silhouette of a '57 Chevy with the bulging headlights and streamlined trunk fins on the back was already a part of American pop culture.

Jimmy Ellis, my 16-year-old neighbor, was sort of famous— and envied—in the neighborhood. He not only had a driver's license, but his first car was a '57 Chevy—a shiny, red, two-door

Chevrolet Bel Air with a V-8 engine. Wherever he drove, it always drew a crowd. "Rev up the motor!" we'd yell. "Spin the tires!"

But Jimmy's Chevy wasn't always so hot. When I first saw the car, Jimmy was still a couple of years away from driving age. And at that point, the car hadn't seen a street or high-school parking lot in a long time.

"Come with me," Jimmy said one afternoon as several of us were taking a break from playing tag football. "You can take a look at my car."

"You've got a car?" several of us asked in unison. He might as well have claimed to own a flying saucer. Car ownership was something we teen mortals could only dream of.

"Watch and learn," Jimmy told us.

We followed him through some woods and down a path, and waded through some tall grass. I was about to conclude that this was some kind of joke when suddenly there it was, surrounded by briars and covered with more rust than paint. Underneath what looked like a hundred years of neglect was the unmistakable outline of a 1957 Chevy Bel Air.

For a few minutes, our small group of teen guys just stood looking over the car. So much potential, but so much to fix! Could the engine ever run again? *How will they ever get this thing out of the woods?* I wondered.

Jimmy broke the reverent silence. "This 1957 Chevy is going to be awesome!" he announced. "My dad and I are gonna give this car a complete restoration."

"A restoration? What's that?" someone asked.

Jimmy looked each of us directly in the eye. "It means that my dad is going to bring this car back from the dead."

## Jesus Is Alive

As awesome as the restoration of a classic car is, a resurrection of a lifeless human body is more impressive. The **resurrection** of Jesus Christ, our fifth core truth, changed history—and eternity—for every human who has ever lived.

Jesus predicted His death and **resurrection** on many occasions. Here are three examples:

### Example 1

From that time on Jesus began to explain to his disciples that he must go to Jerusalem and suffer many things at the hands of the elders, chief priests and teachers of the law, and that he must be killed and on the third day be raised to life. (Matthew 16:21)

### Example 2

When they came together in Galilee, he said to them, "The Son of Man is going to be betrayed into the hands of men. They will kill him, and on the third day he will be raised to life." (Matthew 17:22-23)

### Example 3

Jesus answered them [the Jews], "Destroy this temple, and I will raise it again in three days."

The Jews replied, "It has taken forty-six years to build this temple, and you are going to raise it in three days?" But the temple he had spoken of was his body. After he was raised from the dead, his disciples recalled what he had said. Then they believed the Scripture and the words that Jesus had spoken. (John 2:19-22)

In the texts cited above, Jesus in effect is saying that if you destroy His body, He will raise it up again three days later. Why is Jesus' **resurrection** so crucial? Why do Christians around the world celebrate the empty tomb each Easter? Because Jesus said the **resurrection** would prove that He was the Savior (see Matthew 12:39-40 and Romans 1:4).

## The Resurrection Is the Cornerstone of the Christian Faith

Our key reference for the **resurrection** could be any number of verses in 1 Corinthians 15. Let's focus on verses 3-8, a portion of the New Testament that was written only about three to seven years after Christ's death and **resurrection**:

> For what I received I passed on to you as of first impor-
> tance: that Christ died for our sins according to the Scrip-
> tures, that he was buried, that he was raised on the third day
> according to the Scriptures, and that he appeared to Peter,
> and then to the Twelve. After that, he appeared to more
> than five hundred of the brothers at the same time, most of
> whom are still living. . . . Then he appeared to James, then
> to all the apostles, and last of all he appeared to me also.

What the apostle Paul essentially said is "You want evidence for the **resurrection** of Jesus? Here's your evidence. Ask any of the hundreds of people who saw Him."

Paul then goes on to pin the credibility of his ministry—and of Christianity—on the fact of the **resurrection**:

> And if Christ has not been raised, our preaching is useless and so is your faith. More than that, we are then found to be false witnesses about God, for we have testified about God that he raised Christ from the dead. But he did not raise him if in fact the dead are not raised. For if the dead are not raised, then Christ has not been raised either. And if Christ has not been raised, your faith is futile; you are still in your sins. Then those also who have fallen asleep in Christ are lost. If only for this life we have hope in Christ, we are to be pitied more than all men. But Christ has indeed been raised from the dead. (verses 14-20)

If Jesus had not risen from the dead, then He was just like every other ordinary human. In this passage, the apostle Paul lists six sad conclusions if Jesus had not risen from the dead:

1. Our preaching about Jesus would be worthless. (verses 14 and 17)
2. Our faith in Jesus would be worthless. (verse 14)
3. We Christians are liars. (verse 15)
4. Our sins were not forgiven and we are still guilty. (verse 17)
5. Our loved ones who we thought were saved are not. (verse 18)
6. We have no hope for an afterlife, and in this life we are miserable. (verse 19)

In other words, Christianity utterly falls apart if Jesus is still dead. Scripture, however, practically explodes with words of assurance and comfort:

> But Christ has indeed been raised from the dead.
> (verse 20)

## No More Fear

If Christ has been raised, that gives the Christian hope for an eternal future. We no longer have to live under the curse of sin and spiritual death. In 2 Timothy, Paul explains that his hope and confidence for the future are based on the fact that Jesus "destroyed death" when He rose from the grave (1:10). Interestingly, the word "destroyed" is an ancient word meaning "unemployed." With His power over the grave, Jesus put death out of a job.

That's why a believer in Jesus doesn't have to fear death. Because Jesus rose from the dead, we know that He has the power to do what He says He'll do. Paul expresses great confidence when he writes in verse 12:

> I know whom I have believed, and am convinced
> that he is able to guard what I have entrusted to him
> for that day.

Though we don't know just when it will happen, we all will die one day. Paul is saying, "I know I will stand before God at some point, but I have peace and confidence through the One I have trusted, Jesus." People everywhere shudder at the thought of dying, but Christians are able to face death with peace and assurance. Believers have the promise of everlasting life because of Jesus, who has power over death.

## Exhibit A: The Empty Tomb

Jesus' empty tomb is proof that He was "more than human." As we already discussed in chapters 2 and 5, He was a perfect man and was therefore qualified to die in our place. But because Jesus is also the Son of God, He had the power to come back to life. Fully man, yet fully God—the empty tomb verifies Jesus' unique identity as "God with us."

> "The appearances of Jesus are as well authenticated as anything in antiquity."
> —MICHAEL GREEN, AUTHOR[1]

The fact that Jesus' grave is unoccupied is a convincing detail. An angel pointed this out early that Sunday morning, the first Easter, as several women went to check on the body of Jesus, which had been buried the Friday before:

> "Don't be alarmed," he said. "You are looking for Jesus the Nazarene, who was crucified. He has risen! He is not here. See the place where they laid him." (Mark 16:6)

These are some of the most significant and beautiful words of the New Testament. Several devoted women went to the burial tomb to check on the body of their beloved friend. They were still heartbroken over the gruesome crucifixion that had taken place on Friday.

As the stunned group tried to make sense of the exposed

tomb, the angel emphasized that the place of Jesus' burial was vacant. That angel was the first one ever to point to the empty grave as physical evidence that Jesus was alive.

## Alternative Theories to the Resurrection

The Bible says in Acts 1:3, "After his suffering, he showed himself to these men and gave many convincing proofs that he was alive." But people do not always accept that Jesus rose from the dead just because the Bible says so. Skeptics, doubters, and followers of other religions have raised several alternative theories to explain the empty tomb.

### 1. Jesus Faked His Death

Some skeptics try to explain the empty tomb and **resurrection** with the assumption that Jesus did not really die. "Maybe up on the cross Jesus just acted dead. Maybe He passed out and was presumed dead."

This theory has serious flaws, starting with the fact that crucifixion was not survivable. The Roman soldiers who carried out this torturous method of execution were not about to jeopardize their careers, and possibly their lives, by failing in their duty to kill. Remember, too, that before He was nailed to the cross, Jesus had been severely beaten. His body was already bloodied and weak.

To speculate that Jesus survived the cross—and fooled experienced soldiers into thinking He was dead—is unlikely. To guess that He may have revived in the cold tomb, moved the stone away from the entrance, and then slipped past soldiers guarding the tomb is unrealistic.

Jesus was condemned to die, and Roman authorities made sure that this legal sentence was carried out.

## 2. The Women Went to the Wrong Tomb

The tomb belonged to one of Jesus' followers, Joseph of Arimathea, who stepped forward to handle the burial. Believers in Jerusalem would have known the exact tomb, which had been sealed by a heavy stone (probably weighing 1.5 to 2 tons) and was guarded by Roman soldiers. It's very unlikely that the women went to the wrong tomb.

## 3. The Disciples Stole the Body of Jesus

We've just described how the body of Jesus was secured in the tomb to prevent exactly what some skeptics say could have occurred—that Jesus' disciples stole the body:

> The next day, the one after Preparation Day, the chief priests and the Pharisees went to Pilate. "Sir," they said, "we remember that while he was still alive that deceiver said, 'After three days I will rise again.' So give the order for the tomb to be made secure until the third day. Otherwise, his disciples may come and steal the body and tell the people that he has been raised from the dead. This last deception will be worse than the first."
>
> "Take a guard," Pilate answered. "Go, make the tomb as secure as you know how." So they went and made the tomb secure by putting a seal on the stone and posting the guard. (Matthew 27:62-66)

So there are two huge problems with this theory. First, the Roman soldiers guarding the tomb weren't about to be scared off or overwhelmed by some unarmed Jewish men. And second, stealing the body of Jesus was the last thing on the minds of the disciples, who first and foremost were concerned with their own safety. On the evening of **resurrection** day, they were huddled together behind locked doors "for fear of the Jews" (John 20:19).

## Why Resurrection Matters

Even if Jesus had survived the cross, revived in the cold tomb, moved the stone away from the entrance, and slipped past the soldiers guarding the tomb, skeptics encounter insurmountable problems. Could Jesus' disciples possibly have mistaken this wounded, bloody, barely alive Jesus for a resurrected Jesus? You would have to assume that the disciples willingly engaged in deception, that they went about misleading people. In other words, they lied.

> "As a lawyer, I have made a prolonged study of the evidences for the events of the first Easter. To me, the evidence is absolutely conclusive. Over and over in the court I have secured the verdict on evidences not nearly so compelling."
> —SIR EDWARD CLARK, BRITISH HIGH COURT JUDGE[2]

Jesus had taught His followers to be truthful. If the disciples were telling the world "Jesus arose!" when He had not, then they were telling a lie. Godly Jews knew that the law of Moses included God's command, "You shall not give false testimony against your neighbor" (Exodus 20:16). Jesus affirmed the law God had communicated through Moses, and this portion of it means, "Do not tell lies." It doesn't make sense that the early Christians, who desired to obey Jesus, would have created and spread a message of lies.

On several occasions, Jesus had told His followers—and even His enemies—that His **resurrection** would be the supreme proof that He was the Son of God. It is unthinkable that Jesus Christ, a person who was all about truth, would trick His followers about this. If the disciples were part of a hoax, then they would have been guilty of behavior that was contrary to all that they were taught.

Finally, you have to ask what accounts for the transformed lives of Jesus' disciples. Immediately after having reported seeing Jesus alive, these previously heartbroken, cowardly disciples turned into passionate messengers of the gospel, and nothing they experienced—persecution, prison, and death—got them to change their story or to deny that they had seen Jesus.

Consider this as well: Within a very short time, their consistent preaching that Jesus had conquered death would transform the world. Two men who were initially doubters, James and Paul, became Christians sometime after Jesus' **resurrection**. What happened to change their minds?

*An encounter with the living Jesus.*

Atheists, skeptics, and determined unbelievers have spent years trying to explain away Jesus' **resurrection** with theories, ideas, and speculations. But in order to account for all of the facts, their stories become increasingly more complex and unbelievable.

How much simpler it would be to accept the conclusion that the evidence shows: *God, the One who created the universe and all of life, worked a miracle.* Jesus had come back to life under the power of God, just as He had promised. That's a simple explanation—no theory or fabrication required.

Christianity's opponents could have crushed the early church movement simply by producing a dead body. They didn't because

---

### Bible 911

Erin was a high-school senior when her 50-year-old father died of a heart attack one morning shortly after going to work. At a youth retreat Erin had attended several weeks before her father's death, the daily devotionals had dealt with Jesus' resurrection and what the Bible says about heaven.

"I never really thought about a death happening in my family," Erin explained. "The initial pain and sense of loss was terrible. But all of a sudden, I began to remember the verses we had just studied about the resurrection and heaven. I think the Holy Spirit reminded me of the things we had studied on the retreat."

Erin's family took comfort in the knowledge that her father had been a Christian. She remembers, "I kept thinking about Jesus' words, like, 'Because I live, you also will live,' and 'Do not let your hearts be troubled. Trust in God; trust also in me.'" (See John 14:19 and 14:1.) "I am so glad that our youth group had just studied Jesus' resurrection and His promises about heaven. In the shock of my father's death, these truths were an incredible comfort to me."

they couldn't, and Christianity's opponents in the centuries since then have been no more successful.

## The Biggest News Story of All Time

One day I had the opportunity to visit a city newspaper's printing facility. Down in the basement, I watched in amazement as computers fed stories into gigantic printing presses. Miles of paper flew past at lightning speed across rollers and into cutters and folders.

The last room we visited, a minimuseum, displayed artifacts and antique printing equipment. Framed copies of historic newspapers with famous front-page headlines hung on the walls. Across the room I saw what looked like hundreds of square chunks of metal. Getting closer, I could see that the chunks were letters—lots and lots of old letters stained with ink. The tour guide explained that they were fonts and letters that typesetters formerly loaded by hand onto the presses.

"Every word and every sentence of each page had to be manually typeset," the guide explained. "It took thousands of pieces of text to make up each page."

Some of the fonts were really small, and some were big, maybe one to two inches tall. Then the guide showed me some huge letters that must have been about three inches tall. "These very large letters were used to create front-page headlines for some of the most significant stories of the twentieth century," he explained. I imagined that those larger letters would have been used to break stories like the attack on Pearl Harbor or man walking on the moon.

Then I noticed some really huge letters that looked like they were six or seven inches tall. They also looked as if they had never been used, because they were missing the dried-up ink residue that was clearly visible on the smaller letters.

When I asked the guide which historic newspapers used the largest of all the letters, he said he couldn't recall any headline that large. "Letters this big would have been saved for a really, really big news story. Probably the biggest news story of all time . . . whatever that would be!"

"I can tell you an event that would be worthy of those giant letters," I said. "I know what is the greatest, most significant news event in human history."

"Oh, yeah?" the guide said.

"What about these?" I said. "Here are some choices for the biggest headline of all time":

DEAD MAN COMES BACK TO LIFE!
SON OF GOD CONQUERS THE GRAVE!
THE RISEN JESUS GIVES HOPE TO THE WORLD!

"You may be right," the man said. After a pause he added, "It's too bad they didn't have newspapers back then."

# Core Truth 6: Return

## Christians Believe Jesus Christ Is Coming Again

> *Be patient and **stand** firm, because*
> *the Lord's coming is near.*
>
> —JAMES 5:8

A simple breakfast at a North Carolina truck stop with Daniel Ritchie was one of the more memorable experiences of my life.

"I'll have the pecan pancakes with maple syrup," Daniel said to the waitress.

At the time, Daniel was a high-school junior, and he had asked me to meet with him over breakfast. He had heard me speak on the core truths and wanted to talk with me about how to better understand and defend his faith. We discussed a number of issues—the Bible, Jesus' resurrection, and ancient evidence for the life of Christ.

Daniel also had many questions about biblical prophecy, Christ's **return**, and heaven. "You know, Daniel," I said, "in heaven we get a brand-new body—a perfect resurrection body."

"I know!" he replied. "Believe me, I know. And I'm looking forward to that!"

I was impressed with this young man's intelligence and his eagerness to learn more about God's plan for his life. I was humbled to watch as he carefully cut his stack of pancakes, eating with impeccable manners, drinking both orange juice and coffee—with his *feet*.

Daniel Ritchie was born without arms. As we talked about the great things that will happen when Jesus comes back and our life with the Lord in heaven, Daniel's excitement grew. When Christ **returns**, His work of restoring all things will include a set of arms for my friend.

Because of Daniel and others like him, I better understand why the Bible calls Jesus' **return** "the blessed hope" (Titus 2:13).

## Jesus Is Coming Again

Did you know a human can live about 40 days without food but only eight days without water? Without oxygen, a person can survive for only four minutes.

How long can someone live without hope?

From childhood onward, nagging questions fill our minds: Will I make any friends at my new school? What if I get cut from the team? How am I ever going to pass the end-of-semester exam? What if my parents find out about that speeding ticket? Will I get accepted to the right college, be able to pay my tuition, and get a decent job?

Becoming an adult, earning some income, and getting out on your own can only increase life's worry factor: Should I get married? Whom should I marry? Why didn't I get married? Will I get the promotion I deserve? Will there be more terrorist attacks? Is Social Security really going to be bankrupt by the time I'm too old to work? Could a tsunami hit the West Coast like it did in Thailand? What if I get a terminal illness? What happens after death? Am I ready to meet God?

As a songwriter wrote many years ago, God is faithful in providing for our every need, including "strength for today and bright hope for tomorrow."[1] For the Christian, God's promises are a source of hope that never runs out. And nothing gives greater encouragement to believers than the core truth that Jesus will one day come back to earth.

Just as Jesus entered this world in a special way, His **return** will be a unique event in history, following God's plan precisely. A well-known passage in 1 Thessalonians is our key reference for the **return** of Jesus Christ:

> For the Lord himself [Jesus] will come down from heaven,
> with a loud command, with the voice of the archangel
> and with the trumpet call of God, and the dead in Christ
> will rise first. After that, we who are still alive and are left
> will be caught up together with them in the clouds to
> meet the Lord in the air. And so we will be with the Lord
> forever. (4:16-17)

You could say that the Christian life is all about looking—in four directions: upward, inward, outward, and forward. We look upward, keeping our eyes on God; we look inward, reflecting on our relationship with Jesus Christ; we look outward, seeing people all around us who need Christ; and we look forward to the day we will be with Jesus.

The first chapter of Acts records events that took place after Jesus rose from the grave. Before He officially concluded His first visit as a man on earth, He gave instructions concerning the coming Holy Spirit. His followers then asked, "Lord, are you at this time going to restore the kingdom to Israel?" (1:6).

It was a question concerning promised coming events, and Jesus answered:

> "It is not for you to know the times or dates the Father
> has set by his own authority. But you will receive power
> when the Holy Spirit comes on you; and you will be my
> witnesses in Jerusalem, and in all Judea and Samaria, and
> to the ends of the earth." (1:7-8)

Then Jesus "was taken up before their very eyes, and a cloud hid him from their sight" (1:9). Seconds later, as these Christians were looking up into the sky, two angels appeared and said:

> "Men of Galilee . . . why do you stand here looking into
> the sky? This same Jesus, who has been taken from you
> into heaven, will come back in the same way you have
> seen him go into heaven." (1:11)

It was a reminder that, yes, Jesus will **return**, in the same way that He left—and, in the meantime, you guys have work to do: Get busy with that last command the Master gave you!

Christ's *exit* from the world is closely related to His *entry* back that will happen one day. To be prepared, we are to *witness* and *watch*.

## How's Your Eschatology?

When and how Jesus will come back is part of *eschatology* (*es-ka-TA-lo-gee*), or the study of the end times. Jesus' second coming to earth is a central topic of eschatology, which encompasses the ultimate destiny and purpose of all things. Biblical eschatology touches on all created beings, the world, time, and eternal things.

You should understand eschatology in two senses: general and individual. General eschatology encompasses places and events that are a part of the close of human history. The evil, anti-Christian world system, the **return** of Jesus, the final judgment, and the ushering in of eternity are all subjects related to general eschatology.

Individual (or personal) eschatology deals with the inescapable facts of life, death, and our eternal destiny. These are issues that every person will face—ready or not. According to the Bible, death is more than the mere cessation of bodily functions. Physical death came about as a result of our disobedience to God. But after death comes an unavoidable appointment of judgment before the Almighty God:

> Therefore, just as sin entered the world through one man, and death through sin, and in this way death came to all men, because all sinned. (Romans 5:12)

> For God will bring every deed into judgment, including every hidden thing, whether it is good or evil. (Ecclesiastes 12:14)

In its coverage of end-time events and future judgment, the Bible does not teach that people get a second chance after death or experience reincarnation (see Hebrews 9:27-28).

Christ's **return** touches on both general and individual eschatologies. It affects the general events of the world by ushering in an end to the human race as we know it. It affects the individual because at that point each person will be judged.

When Jesus was on earth 2,000 years ago, He predicted His **return**, which would take place at some future point. He said to the disciples:

> "At that time the sign of the Son of Man will appear in the sky, and all the nations of the earth will mourn. They will see the Son of Man coming on the clouds of the sky, with power and great glory." (Matthew 24:30)

## I.V.D.A.R.R.

Need help remembering the six core beliefs? Here's a simple memory device: Use the funny word IVDARR. It stands for

**I**nspiration

**V**irgin Birth

**D**eity of Christ

**A**tonement

**R**esurrection

**R**eturn of Christ

The early church leaders, and Christians throughout history, have taken great comfort in the promise of Christ's **return**. Christians have the promise that one day this chaotic world will be brought into line with God's perfect plan.

## Something New?

As we've already seen in several Bible passages, the triumphant **return** of Christ is not a new teaching—at least not for Christians who take the Bible seriously. People who reject the idea of the Second Coming have a problem with biblical prophecy. They don't believe that the Bible can accurately predict the future.

For 2,000 years, however, Christian leaders have taught and commented on what the Bible says about future events, including the second coming of Christ. Between the years of A.D. 30 and 430, church fathers held views similar to some of today's leaders. They include: Clement of Rome (30-95), Polycarp (70-155), Ignatius (35-107), Papius (80-163), Justin Martyr (100-164), Cyprian (200-258), and Augustine (354-430).

I know that you're probably not familiar with these names, but the point is that for many centuries godly followers of Jesus have believed He would make a second visit to earth.

Around A.D. 150 (only about 55 years after the final book of the New Testament was written), Justin Martyr wrote an explanation and defense of the faith. It was the longest, most extensive Christian work at the time. Here is one paragraph from Justin Martyr's writings:

Moreover also a man among us named John, one of the
apostles of Christ, prophesied in a revelation made to
him that those who believed on our Christ will spend a
thousand years in Jerusalem; and that hereafter the general
and, in short, the eternal resurrection and judgment of all
will likewise take place.[2]

Note that he affirms John's authority as one who was actually with Jesus. Justin Martyr is also recognizing John's "revelation" (this vision from God, which John was told to write; see
Revelation 1:1, 11, and 19). He mentions the millennial
(1,000-year) reign of Christ and God's final judgment of all
people.

It's been said that God's written revelation—the entire Bible,
which "reveals" the mind of God—is perfect, yet partial. God
didn't tell us every miniuscule detail about the future. But the
important facts that believers have agreed upon are that Christ
will **return**, will judge the world in righteousness, and will usher
in His eternal kingdom.

Let us then wait for the kingdom of God from hour to
hour in love and righteousness, seeing that we know not
the day of the appearing of God. —Clement of Rome,
A.D. 30-95[3]

## Why Jesus' Return Matters

Does any Christian have complete understanding of every detail
about the end times? I don't think so. Godly, gifted, and good

Christians have often disagreed about certain specific details related to prophecy. There are many good books available presenting various views on Bible prophecy.

I think the Lord desires that we study Bible prophecy carefully and prayerfully. Think about this: When it came to including predictions and prophecy in the Bible, God certainly did not hold back. An estimated 25 percent to 30 percent of the Bible is prophetic. We've graciously been given a lot of information about future events.

But also consider the only book of prophecy in the New Testament, Revelation, which contains much information on the **return** of Christ. Revelation makes a unique promise in its very first chapter:

[Happy] is the one who reads the words of this prophecy, and blessed are those who hear it and take to heart what is written in it, because the time is near. (1:3)

People care about future events. Christians can help others understand and have hope that Jesus' **return** will bring righteousness and healing for believers. While in a bank one day, I noticed that the teller handling my transaction kept glancing over at a television in the lobby. As images of desert warfare flashed across the screen, she said, "Every day I wonder what this world is coming to!"

I smiled and repeated the saying, "The question is not, 'What is the world coming to?' The important thing is 'Who's coming to the world!'"

The teller paused, looked across the desk, and asked, "Are

you talking about Jesus coming back? Can you tell me what the Bible says about that?"

Knowledge of Christ's sudden **return** is not only an incentive for faithfulness in your personal walk with the Lord; it's also an

---

### What Jesus Says About His Return in Matthew

- Jesus presides over final judgment in "that day" (7:21-23)
- Jesus gathers (and judges) the entire human race (13:41-43)
- Jesus commissions angels to separate the wicked from the just (13:49-50)
- Son of Man comes in glory (16:27)
- Son of Man sits on the throne of glory (19:28)
- Son of Man comes like lightning from the sky (24:27-31)
- Son of Man comes at an unexpected time (24:36-44)
- Jesus says to "be prepared" for His return (25:1-13)
- Son of Man comes in glory, judges the nations (25:31-46)
- Son of Man comes sitting at the right hand of heavenly power (26:64)

### What Jesus Says About His Return in Mark

- Son of Man is ashamed of those who were ashamed of Him (8:38)
- Son of Man comes, chosen ones are gathered from every direction (13:26-27)

evangelism tool in your personal witness. Many people want to know what the Bible has to say. Believers should be able and willing to provide a simple explanation of things related to the Christian faith.

- Son of Man is like one gone on a long journey, whose time of return is unknown (13:34-37)
- Son of Man is God and will return in power and on clouds (14:62)

### What Jesus Says About His Return in Luke

- Son of Man comes at a certain time period, so we should "watch" (12:35-40)
- Son of Man returns as quickly as lightning, at some future point after His crucifixion and resurrection (17:24-25)
- Christ returns (21:25-28)
- Christ's return is as rapid as a trap snapping shut, so do not be conformed to the characteristics of this sinful world (21:34-36)

### What Jesus Says About His Return in John

- Christ comes again after having prepared a place for believers (14:1-4)
- Christ comes again, undetermined time of return is implied (21:22-23)

He who testifies to these things says, "Yes, I am coming soon" (Revelation 22:20).

Remember the passage from 1 Thessalonians 4? The description of Christ's **return** is followed by this challenge in verse 18: "Therefore encourage each other with these words."

Knowledge that we will see our Savior—maybe today—is an inspiration for faithful living. God doesn't let us in on every detail about tomorrow, but we are plainly told that Jesus will be back. Matthew 24 records Jesus' teaching a group of His followers about future events. Christians have endlessly discussed how to apply the teaching of this prophetic chapter, but a couple of principles come through clearly. Jesus impressed on His followers that they should watch, and be ready, "because you do not know on what day your Lord will come" (Matthew 24:42).

Christian, be continuously on guard.

# EIGHT

# The Gospel Stands—No Matter What "They" Say!

*The plans of the LORD **stand** firm forever,*
*the purposes of his heart through all generations.*
—Psalm 33:11

Early in the twentieth century, a Michigan lawyer was given the opportunity to invest in a new business by an inventor who promised a large return. When the lawyer asked his banker for five thousand dollars, the bank president asked what the money would be used for. The attorney explained that he would be investing in the design and construction of "motorized carriages."

The banker refused the lawyer's request, saying, "One day you'll thank me for declining this loan." But the resolute attorney ignored the advice and eventually scraped together enough money to invest in the upstart business.

He made the right decision. In less than 10 years, his five-thousand-dollar investment was worth $12.5 million. The attorney's investment had become valuable stock in the Ford Motor Company. What the banker said would be worthless turned out to be a substantial fortune.[1]

In many ways, Christianity is like that. Some people assume that believing in God, trusting the Bible, and following Jesus is a waste of one's life. But a life invested in the things of God yields priceless benefits. Skeptics may scoff at Christianity, and critics tear into the Bible, but the message of Jesus—unchanged after 2,000 years—still wins hearts and minds.

We have just completed a brief look at six core truths of Christianity. You may have noticed, however, that the world doesn't define truth the way the Bible does. Every day the Christian faith is hammered on and beaten up in the media—and probably at your school, too. In this chapter, I want to show you that the gospel stands even when challenged in the following seven ways.

## Seven Reasons the Gospel Stands, Even When It's Pushed Around

Don't get discouraged as you represent Christ in this pluralistic, tolerant, alternative-lifestyle, twenty-first-century world! Stand for Christ even if it seems as if you are standing alone. You are not alone; the Lord Almighty is with you. And remember, Christianity is still authentic, genuine, and true regardless of the following:

### 1. Regardless of the critical person's prestige
All of the skeptics in the world, regardless of their degrees and academic achievements, cannot argue Christianity into falseness.

Jesus remains the risen Lord and door to heaven, despite what anyone may say.

Let me be clear: I am for education. But sadly, the academic world has become a consistently hostile environment for Christianity. Over the years, many distraught teens and college students have come to me with questions and comments like: "My teachers at college seem really smart, and they said that Jesus never claimed to be God. My professor says that truth is relative [whatever that means], and that all beliefs are equally valid."

Famous media personalities also often slam Christianity. For example, Mark Burnett, producer of *Survivor* and *The Apprentice,* said:

> I don't believe in any religion. It's all made up. Religion is an organized thing by human beings to convince other people to follow a way of speaking to God. I think God's in everybody, and you have to be in touch with yourself and your god within you.[2]

Just because someone is rich and famous doesn't mean he or she knows the truth about God.

The critic of Christianity may not just be someone on TV—it may be someone you see every day or even someone you admire. The critic's objections may relate to only one or to dozens of issues regarding God and Christianity. The key is to identify why that person's opinion matters to you. Try this little exercise and fill in the blanks to find out who in your life is criticizing the Bible.

"But my _____(teacher—friend—boss)
who has a _____(Ph.D.—lots of friends—million
dollars) says that _____" (the Bible is
wrong—the Bible is just a myth—all religions lead to
heaven)

So, some who are rich, popular, or famous have opinions
about God that contradict the Bible. Don't get discouraged—it
really doesn't matter. What does matter is what God thinks. Let
me remind you that God has given us an assessment about those
rich, famous, popular, or scholarly people who deny Him:

> For the message of the cross is foolishness to those who
> are perishing, but to us who are being saved it is the
> power of God. . . . For the wisdom of this world is fool-
> ishness in God's sight. (1 Corinthians 1:18, 3:19)
>     What if some did not have faith? Will their lack of
> faith nullify God's faithfulness? Not at all! Let God be
> true, and every man a liar. (Romans 3:3-4)

Christians are to accept the revelation of God over the opinions of men. Remember it is the Word of God that stands the test
of time:

> "All men are like grass, and all their glory is like the flow-
> ers of the field; the grass withers and the flowers fall, but
> the word of the Lord stands forever." (1 Peter 1:24-25)

Respect people in positions of authority and power. Be
friendly to non-Christian teens—but look to God for truth.

## 2. Regardless of the number of voices raised in opposition

I hear objections to the Bible on a regular basis, especially when I speak on college campuses. If I make a statements like, "Jesus said that He was the only way to God, and only through Him may we experience heaven and avoid hell," members of the audience will say, "Nobody believes that anymore." Everybody today accepts all viewpoints—except Christianity; they believe real virtue is tolerance and that no one book or person or group has a corner on truth.

Remember that the message of God is true, regardless of how many people may or may not believe it. Truth is in no way tied to the numbers of human beings who recognize it.

> "No one ever graduates from Bible study until they meet the Author face to face."
> —EVERTT HARRIS[3]

Popular opinion may say that Christianity is out of date, but popular opinion is often wrong. There was a time when many people thought that the world was flat. In the mid-1800s, many doctors in America thought that tomatoes were poison and encouraged people not to eat them. Such popular ideas were wrong!

Remember that truth is true, even if no one believes it. Error is wrong even if everyone believes it.

## 3. Regardless of the length of time unbelief has persisted

After speaking on Christianity at a college, I met a young woman who said, "You know, the oldest of the world's religions is Wicca."

"That's debatable," I said. "The term *Wicca* has been around only since the 1950s."

"But it is true," she said, "that witchcraft has been around for thousands of years."

My response to that is a hearty "So what?" False religions have existed for centuries. Does truth have an expiration date? No. Jesus will still be Lord and His Word will still be true regardless of the length of time that unbelief exists.

Truth is timeless. What God has said will not go out of date. If God's Word *was* true (and God cannot lie), then what God communicated to man still *is* true.

Human unbelief may persist for centuries. No problem. Disbelief says more about human nature than it does about divine revelation.

### 4. Regardless of the argument's sophistication

Scholarly objections against the Bible can be complex. False religions often present themselves as being "better" than Christianity, more tolerant, more sophisticated, more beneficial.

Christianity has been opposed in ways that range from the simple to the complex. Don't let the sophistication of someone's argument lead you to doubt the truth of Christ. People have questioned God's truth in various ways for various reasons.

> "Never doubt in the dark what God has shown you in the light."
> —RAYMOND EDMAN[4]

I am not saying that all nonbelievers are calculatingly evil. Not at all. Some people have honest questions for which they are seeking answers. Other people, for whatever reason, may not want Christianity to be true. Some have spent great amounts of mental energy trying to think up arguments against Christianity. One man plainly told me he resisted coming to Christ because it meant he would have to give up some behavior he knew was wrong.

The Bible and the message of Jesus have been questioned and denied by various people, for various reasons, and with different degrees of complexity. In the minds of some, God is guilty until proven innocent. But humans weren't the first ones to cross-examine what God has said.

Satan was the world's first Scripture twister. He was the first to try to persuade others to reject what God had clearly said. Then and now, Satan has opposed the message of God in skillful and complex ways. Throughout the Bible we read of the devil distorting and denying God's own words.

Consider how Satan misused the Bible in his temptation of Adam and Eve. The conversation is very interesting:

> Now the serpent was more crafty than any of the wild animals the LORD God had made. He said to the woman, "Did God really say, 'You must not eat from any tree in the garden'?"
>
> The woman said to the serpent, "We may eat fruit from the trees in the garden, but God did say, 'You must not eat fruit from the tree that is in the middle of the garden, and you must not touch it, or you will die.'"
>
> "You will not surely die," the serpent said to the woman. "For God knows that when you eat of it your eyes will be opened, and you will be like God, knowing good and evil." (Genesis 3:1-5)

I believe that Satan carefully chose his words to cause Adam and Eve to turn from God. Follow the line of thought that takes place:

| Statement or implication: | Mental/spiritual result: |
|---|---|
| "Did God really say?" (verse 1) | doubt |
| "God didn't really say . . ." (verse 4) | denial |
| "What God really meant was . . ." (verse 5) | deception |
| "What you ought to do instead is . . ." (verses 5-6) | disobedience |
| "Trust me, you won't die! Your eyes will be opened." (verse 5) | death (sin, separation from God) |

Proverbs 14:12 warns, "There is a way that seems right to a man, but in the end it leads to death." There are several causes of unbelief. People may be one of the following:

**Biased**— "I won't believe in Jesus."
**Searching**— "I'd be open to belief if I could understand _____."
**Uninformed**— "I didn't know this about Jesus."

Christians must prepare to respond effectively both to honest questions and baseless objections.

### 5. Regardless of scientific discoveries
In Paris's Louvre museum there is a library with three and a half miles of bookshelves that hold thousands of science books. What's unusual about these "science" books is that they are already outdated. The books were thought to be accurate in their day but are now known to contain incorrect information. This collection serves as a historical curiosity, proof that even learned humans make volumes of mistakes.

Dr. H. L. Willmington of Liberty University explains that it is always premature to assume that man's ideas have surpassed God's truth:

> In 1861, the French Academy of Science produced a brochure of fifty-one Scientific Facts which supposedly contradicted the Bible. These were used by atheists of the day in ridiculing Christians. Today, all fifty-one of those facts are unacceptable to modern scientists.[5]

Be patient, Bible-believing friend. The cracks in the theories of naturalism and evolution are beginning to show; you may see the foundation crumble in your lifetime. Time and again the Christian's trust in the Bible has been proven sound while popular science has been refuted.

### 6. Regardless of Christian hypocrisy

What has turned more people into atheists than all of the textbooks on evolution in the world? Why do many people forsake church for cults? If some surveys of nonbelievers are accurate (and I think that they are), what is the number-one thing that makes those outside of the faith reject Jesus?

Christian hypocrisy.

Consider the words of tobyMac, a Grammy-winning artist from the band dcTalk:

> The single biggest cause of atheism is Christians who acknowledge Jesus with their lips but walk out the door and deny him with their lifestyle.[6]

Atheists frequently point out that Christians sometimes aren't very Christlike. Muslims, who believe it's a great sin to show disrespect to elders, cringe at the way some American teens speak to their parents. Many homosexuals point to the actions and attitudes of some Christians as reason for their dislike of the church.

People who have non-Christian (and even anti-Christian) attitudes have told me things like: "The pastor at a local church was caught viewing online pornography. What's up with that?" "Some of the people who are always inviting me to their church youth group are the same guys I know who drink and party more than anybody else on the weekends."

The sad part is that nonbelievers are right—the church "talks it" but doesn't always "walk it." And that is the number-one complaint by those who resist the gospel.

> *Some people look at the way things are and ask, "Why?" Others look at the way things could be and ask, "Why not?"*
> —AMERICAN PROVERB

People who represent Christ should be godly people of a higher standard. But the failures of Christians do not mean that the gospel isn't true. It is unfortunate that our actions could tarnish the image of Christ in the minds of people. But the Christian message remains real and relevant, even when we don't represent it as well as we should.

With the Lord's help we should strive to be the most appealing, most magnetic witnesses possible. Titus 2:10 challenged a group of believers to behavior that would "make the teaching about God our Savior attractive."

The good news of Jesus should be carried forth by godly messengers. But Christianity's truth and accuracy are always consistent, even if the church that represents it isn't.

## 7. *Regardless of Christian apathy*

We Christians have been trusted with an important mission. Sometimes the church doesn't appear concerned that souls without Jesus are really lost. Sometimes it seems that believers have forgotten that God expects the Bible to be cherished and obeyed. Why is it important to preserve the purity of the message? Because of the gospel's *origin* and *urgency*.

We need to seriously consider that the *origin* of the Bible is God. (Remember chapter 2?) He is the author. Galatians 1:11 reminds us:

> I want you to know, brothers, that the gospel I preached is not something that man made up.

We also need to act with a sense of *urgency*. Souls are at stake. Christians can sometimes get slack in their appreciation for God's Word. Believers may occasionally need their compassion for lost souls rekindled.

The gospel is true, relevant, and—in light of man's spiritual condition—urgent. Yet believers may sometimes get their priorities out of order, and reaching others for Christ may lose its importance.

The apostle Paul in 2 Timothy 4:2-4 challenged us:

> Preach the Word; be prepared in season and out of season; correct, rebuke and encourage—with great patience and careful instruction. For the time will come when men will

not put up with sound doctrine. Instead, to suit their own desires, they will gather around them a great number of teachers to say what their itching ears want to hear. They will turn their ears away from the truth and turn aside to myths.

### How Many Animals Did Moses Take on the Ark?

Did you know "Jesus wept" is the shortest verse in the Bible? Maybe not, if you're like the average U.S. teen. A 2005 Gallup Poll found that nearly two-thirds of teens didn't recognize Jesus' most famous address, the Sermon on the Mount. Only one in 10 knew who Moses was. (Noah was on the ark; Moses received the Ten Commandments.)

To get a basic Bible foundation, you don't have to go to Bible college or even a formal Bible study. While those organized study settings are great, they aren't necessary to begin learning about the Bible. All you have to do is read it.

Knowing Bible basics can also give you an academic edge, according to a survey of high-school English teachers by the Bible Literature Project in Fairfax, Virginia.[7] Like Shakespearian literature, biblical allusions and quotes are part of our cultural heritage. You should be able to understand what it means when someone uses terms from the Bible like "forbidden fruit" or "prodigal son."

But you should also read the Bible for another reason—it can give you a spiritual edge, an intimate understanding of the heart of God.

How well those verses describe today's culture. The message of the gospel is urgent. Only God knows how long our culture has before those in it will turn aside from the truth completely.

Now that you have studied the six core truths of Christianity and can shake off the seven most common arguments against believing the Bible, you're ready for the next chapter: "Stand."

# NINE

# Stand

***Stand** firm. Let nothing move you. Always give yourselves fully to the work of the Lord, because you know that your labor in the Lord is not in vain.*

—1 CORINTHIANS 15:58

Legend has it that a French town was known for its larger-than-life statue of Jesus. During World War II, the figure of Christ was damaged in a bombing raid, and both hands were broken off. The town hired a master sculptor to repair the Jesus statue. When the townspeople came to see his progress, however, the hands had not been replaced.

Instead the sculptor had created a plaque with an inscription that read, "He has no hands but our hands."

If we don't do the work of Christ, who will?

Dr. Billy Graham, the world-famous evangelist mentioned in chapter 1, knew that preaching wasn't enough. A Christian has to live like Christ. Dr. Graham wrote:

The power to proclaim the greatest news in heaven and earth was not given to the angels; it was given to redeemed men. Every Christian is to be a witness; every follower of Christ is to preach the Gospel. We can preach by sharing our experiences with others. We can preach by exalting Christ in our daily lives. Sermons which are seen are often more effective than those which are heard. The truth is, the best sermons are both heard and seen.[1]

## My Role as a Christian

If people are going to hear about Christ, the Christians who know them must speak up. The world looks for God, so they should see Jesus in our lives. The Bible says that believers make up Christ's body (1 Corinthians 12:12-27). The wise sculptor knew that Christians are to serve as Jesus' hands—and we are also to be His feet, arms, eyes, and voice.

We can also show love as if we had God's heart. The Christian is a representative of Christ—where ever and whenever. Second Corinthians 5:20 makes the point clear:

We are therefore Christ's ambassadors, as though God were making his appeal through us.

## Love Christ by Loving Others

I encourage you to "keep the fire" and maintain a consistent, passionate, fruitful walk with the Lord! Don't get bored with God, and don't forget that someone loved His Word enough to pass the message on to *you*. The Bible says that the gospel is "good news," and I would add that it is still *news*.

There is an old song about not growing tired of the message of Jesus. It is titled "I Love to Tell the Story." Its words are an appropriate cure for the apathy that we can all fall into:

I love to tell the story; more wonderful it seems
Than all the golden fancies of all our golden dreams.
I love to tell the story, it did so much for me;
And that is just the reason I tell it now to thee.

I love to tell the story; 'tis pleasant to repeat
What seems, each time I tell it, more wonderfully sweet.
I love to tell the story, for some have never heard
The message of salvation from God's own holy Word.

I love to tell the story, for those who know it best
Seem hungering and thirsting to hear it like the rest.
And when, in scenes of glory, I sing the new, new song,
'Twill be the old, old story that I have loved so long.

I love to tell the story, 'twill be my theme in glory,
To tell the old, old story of Jesus and His love.[2]

### Building a Solid Foundation

While on a business trip to Florida, I took a tour of the Vehicle Assembly Building at the Kennedy Space Center. The steel pipe piles *beneath* it were driven into the earth about 160 feet, where they rest on rock. Many years ago, as engineers calculated and designers planned the space center, it was determined that *the higher you plan to reach, the deeper your foundation must be.*

Depth and height are also related in the Christian's walk. Reaching great heights for the Lord requires depth in your daily Christian walk. Would you like to really make a mark for the name of Jesus? You can do it! God will help you. Billy Graham said, "The disciples were able to turn the world upside down, because their hearts had been turned right side up."[3]

Yours can be a life that will count for all of eternity, but it won't happen by accident. Reading the Bible, studying, praying, memorizing, sharing consistently—such things require discipline. Will it be easy? Not really. But would it be right? Absolutely.

### *Reaching Our Friends for Christ*

You may not know who Albert McMakin was, but God used this individual in a great way. In 1934, he was a 24-year-old farm worker who wanted to see his friends come to faith in Christ. When a traveling evangelist came preaching nearby, Albert began to take people to the services in his truck.

One of the young men whom Albert wanted to reach for Christ was the son of a local dairy farmer. But the youth did not seem interested at all. Sports, girls, and other things seemed to occupy the young man's attention.

Albert was persistent, however, and the friend eventually agreed to come to the evangelistic event, and the group rode together in Albert's truck. After hearing the speaker and coming back to the services for several nights, the young man began to think seriously about his relationship to God.

In one of the services, Albert's friend responded to the invitation and opened his heart to Christ. You may have already guessed it, but the friend was Billy Graham, and this was the service where he first heard the evangelist Mordecai Hamm (as mentioned in chapter 1). Albert McMakin is an example for believers; we need to faithfully reach out on behalf of Christ and watch God bring about wonderful results. It took a team, the "body of Christ," to reach Billy Graham, but Albert McMakin started the chain of events by doing his part.[4]

### Keep the Faith, but Not to Yourself!

Standing for God in this world requires patience, consistency, and wisdom. God told His followers to present His message to the world, and He promised to provide the resources needed for the job:

> "But you will receive power when the Holy Spirit comes
> on you; and you will be my witnesses in Jerusalem, and
> in all Judea and Samaria, and to the ends of the earth."
> (Acts 1:8)

God's Word presents a *personal walk* and *visible witness* as an everyday part of being a Christian:

> Day after day, in the temple courts and from house to
> house, they never stopped teaching and proclaiming the
> good news that Jesus is the Christ. (Acts 5:42)

James 1:5 contains a promise that Christians should remember when they pray:

If any of you lacks wisdom, he should ask God, who gives generously to all without finding fault, and it will be given to him.

May God equip our hearts and heads to share this with the world.

### Do the Best You Can with What You've Got

The Lord has given each of us time, talents, treasure, and testimony. We have the privilege (and, really, the obligation) to invest these resources into things that will bring good to people and glory to God. By remembering that all we have and are comes from the Lord, we will be compelled to offer it back to Him in sacrifice. In his autobiography, *Be My Guest*, Conrad Hilton observed that a bar of iron (in his day) was worth five dollars. If that same bar of iron was made into horseshoes, it would be worth $10.80. If that same quantity of iron was made into sewing needles, the resulting product would be worth $3,200. If that same amount of iron was made into mainsprings for wristwatches, the result would have a value of $250,000.[5] This illustration shows that the final value is determined by what you do with what you're given. As Christians we have been given different abilities and gifts; what we ultimately become is determined not by what we have but by how we use what we have.

### Church: "The Most Exciting Place in Town"?

You may have heard of the little boy who entertained himself during worship by staring at plaques hung on the walls of the sanctuary. He asked his mother why all of the names had been recorded and displayed. She replied, "Those were the people who died in the service." The little boy thought for a moment and asked, "Which service? Did they die in the 8:30 service or in the 11:00 service?"

Church and worship should not be like Chinese water torture, though they may prompt similar feelings in some people. "The preacher at our church reminds me of Moses and Pharaoh," complained one man. "The service makes me want to shout, 'Let my people go!' "

One time at a youth event, a teenager was telling me about a concert she had attended the night before: "It was, like, only the most exciting thing *in history.*"

I asked the girl and her friends a question: "If the concert was at the top, then on a scale of one to 10, how would you rate your church and youth group?"

The girls exchanged glances and giggled to themselves. One teen responded, "Church is okay. . . . I mean, church is a good thing." The other girls backed her up, nodding in emphatic agreement.

But "concert girl" qualified the compliment: "A lot of words could be used to describe this church, but *exciting* isn't one of them."

Going to church can be thought of as boring; no news flash there. But in reality, no other enterprise on planet Earth has a profile that even comes close to that of the church. Consider these facts about the church:

> **The founder and leader:** God Himself.
> **The organization's duration:** Spanning the centuries.
> **Its mission:** To deliver a communiqué handed down from heaven.

**The content of this message:** Timeless truth in a world of error.

**The validity of its message:** Authentic in a world of pretenders.

**The results of its message:** Truly life changing in an otherwise hopeless world.

**The church's importance:** Vital, affecting the eternal destiny of souls.

**Its power source:** The third person of the Trinity, God the Holy Spirit.

**Its labor force:** Countless believers from every time and place.

**Commitment requirement:** Total; you must give up your life.

**Risk level:** The main risk comes only if you are less than 100 percent committed.

**Support from upper management:** Divine.

**Its compensation structure:** Absolutely unequalled here and hereafter. In this life, each Christian gets forgiveness, meaning, purpose, fulfillment, peace, assurance, and life long enrichment in a number of areas. In the next life, you miss hell and get heaven, a mansion, rewards beyond human description, enjoyment of God's presence. Plus you'll have all of eternity to mix and mingle with the heroes of history, who, like yourself, rose up and made their mark in the world as part of God's great story.

First Corinthians 6:19 tells us that each individual believer is the temple (dwelling place) of God. So you, Christian, are *the church.* The word "church" can mean a lot of things. But it shouldn't mean "boring."

Reflect on the following observations:

> I am part of God's church on earth today.
> I am part of the believers who have existed throughout history.
> I am someone who has been given an assignment by almighty God.

G. K. Chesterton compared truth (that is, God's revealed truth, or the Christian worldview) to a white stallion that has run throughout history. Some people have welcomed this white horse of truth while others have fired arrows at it, tried to drive it away, or even tried to kill it.

Chesterton explains that at the end of time, after Satan and all of the opponents of God have been defeated, the "white horse of truth" will remain. When the smoke of Armageddon clears, as enemies of God lie scattered around, out from the mist emerges the "white horse of truth, wounded, scarred, perhaps bloody. But standing tall, nonetheless."[6]

God calls us to stand, also. We are to lovingly, consistently, patiently, stand tall each day as representatives of our Lord. Will this always be easy or convenient? No. Will standing up for God always make us popular? Not really. Will there be times of discouragement and self-doubt? Yes. Remember that people whom God uses the most often endure very rough times and periods of great struggle. But will Jesus be the faithful friend and guardian who carries us along every single day? Definitely.

God calls us to stand, but He doesn't expect us to live the victorious Christian life in our own strength. God doesn't send us out to touch the world via our own abilities.

Ephesians 6 contains some great information about the life of visible and vocal witness that we each are called to live. God's Word reminds us that we are involved in spiritual battle—and like any wise soldier, we don't go onto the field until we put on armor:

> Finally, be strong in the Lord and in his mighty power. Put on the full armor of God so that you can take your stand against the devil's schemes. For our struggle is not against flesh and blood, but against the rulers, against the authorities, against the powers of this dark world and against the spiritual forces of evil in the heavenly realms. Therefore put on the full armor of God, so that when the day of evil comes, you may be able to **stand** your ground, and after you have done everything, to **stand**. **Stand** firm then, with the belt of truth buckled around your waist, with the breastplate of righteousness in place, and with your feet fitted with the readiness that comes from the gospel of peace. In addition to all this, take up the shield of faith, with which you can extinguish all the flaming arrows of the evil one. Take the helmet of salvation and the sword of the Spirit, which is the word of God. And pray in the Spirit on all occasions with all kinds of prayers and requests. With this in mind, be alert and always keep on praying for all the saints.
>
> Pray also for me, that whenever I open my mouth, words may be given me so that I will fearlessly make

known the mystery of the gospel, for which I am an ambassador in chains. Pray that I may declare it fearlessly, as I should. (verses 10-20, emphasis added)

The people of God can stand, because the truths of God stand. Individually and collectively, today, tomorrow, and always—God's message and His messengers *stand.* Ephesians 6:10 reminds us to find our strength in God's power and presence. Ephesians 6 compares some different aspects of the Christian life to a soldier's battle armor. With vivid clarity, the text illustrates our need for Christ's presence in all areas of life.

Appropriate military gear is essential in protecting the soldier's vulnerable body parts (like the chest, heart, lungs, head, and limbs). If we desire God's strength, presence, and protection, He promises to faithfully provide these things.

Truth and righteousness are like supportive and protective armor (verse 14). In verse 15 the message of Jesus is compared to protective footgear (the gospel brings peace in this world—peace with God, and peace with each other). Faith (which literally means "trust") is compared to a shield, which deflects the ammunition of Satan (see verse 16). Protection of a soldier's head and brain is of critical importance, and verse 17 compares salvation to a helmet of safety. For the Christian, guarding the mind (thoughts, beliefs, emotions) is as important as physically guarding the brain itself.

For this reason, knowledge of Scripture is vitally important. Ephesians 6:17 refers to the Word of God as a sword, given by the Holy Spirit. Soldiers going into battle without a sword would find themselves in a life-threatening situation. Similarly a Christian who is unfamiliar with the Word of God will eventually find himself in a position of extreme vulnerability. Truly the Bible's value in the life of the Christian cannot be overestimated!

Finally verse 18 reminds us of the importance of prayer. For the Christian who goes the distance—the one who follows Christ and remains standing to the end—prayer will be a key ingredient. Ephesians 6:18 links our consistency and perseverance to our prayer life. There is an important connection between time spent with God in prayer and the Christian's victory in the battles of life.

Sometimes believers start out standing tall for Christ and later end up fallen. Though the failures of Christians do not change the truth of the gospel (see chapter 8), it is unfortunate that this has often been one of the main objections to the gospel raised by nonbelievers. Having debated on campuses and engaged in many radio dialogues with skeptics, I can attest to the fact that atheists and skeptics delight in pointing out that sometimes the people of God are very ungodly.

But God's design and plan are that you stand tall for Him. And God's Word assures us that it can be done. The vivid pictures of Ephesians 6 remind us of the promises that, having taken on the armor of God, we may withstand life's challenges. Verse 13 is a conclusion that we would all like our lives to reflect—"and after you have done everything, to stand."

At the end of your journey, whenever that may come, you can look back knowing that with the Lord's help, you stood. In taking a stand for the Lord Jesus Christ your life will have counted for something eternal.

**Notes**

## Chapter 1: How to Understand the Six Core Truths of Christianity

1. The Barna Group, "Born Again Christians," http://www.barna.org/FlexPage.aspx?Page=Topic&TopicID=8, May 13, 2005.

2. "Former LDS Leader Concerned over Protestant Embrace of Mormon Beliefs" Truth Talk Live radio broadcast. Truth Broadcasting Network (Winston Salem, N.C., April 11, 2003).

3. Jerome, quoted in Mark Water, *Hard Questions About the Bible Made Easy* (Peabody, Mass.: Hendrickson Publishers, 2000), p. 25.

4. Mordecai Hamm, quoted by Dr. Alvin Reid, North Carolina Conference of Vocational Baptist Evangelists, (Asheboro, N.C., January 2000).

5. Billy Graham Evangelistic Association, "About Us: Biographies," http://www.billygraham.org/media Relations/bios.asp?p=1, May 31, 2005.

## Chapter 2: Inspiration

1. Dan Brown, *The Da Vinci Code* (New York: Random House, 2003), p. 235.

2. Harold Willmington, *That Manuscript from Outer Space* (Nashville: Thomas Nelson, 1977), p. 86. See also Earle

E. Cairns, *Christianity Through the Centuries* (Grand Rapids, Mich.: Zondervan, 1996), p. 92.

3. Harold Willmington, *Willmington's Guide to the Bible*, (Wheaton, Ill.: Tyndale, 1988) p. 813.

4. Neil Altman, "Revisionist Scholars seek to alter Biblical Texts," *Jewish News*, April 22, 2005.

5. Norman L. Geisler and Frank Turek, *I Don't Have Enough Faith to Be an Atheist* (Wheaton, Ill.: Crossway, 2004), p. 228.

6. Hans von Kampenhausen, quoted in Gary R. Habermas, *The Historical Jesus: Ancient Evidence for the Life of Christ* (Joplin, Mo.: College Press, 1996), p. 156.

7. F. F. Bruce, *The New Testament Documents—Are They Reliable?* (Downers Grove, Ill.: InterVarsity Press, 1971), p. 15.

8. J. I. Packer, *God Speaks to Man* (Philadelphia: The Westminster Press, 1965), p. 81.

9. Anonymous, quoted in Erwin W. Lutzer, *7 Reasons You Can Trust the Bible* (Chicago.: Moody Press, 1998), p. 31.

10. Martin Luther, quoted by H. L. Willmington, *That Manuscript from Outer Space* (Nashville: Thomas Nelson, 1977), p. 38.

## Chapter 3: Virgin Birth

1. Joseph Mohr and Franz Gruber, "Silent Night! Holy Night!" (p.d.). *Hymns of the Christian Life*, (Harrisburg, Pa.: Christian Publications, Inc., 1936) p. 64.

2. William Arndt and F. Wilbur Gingrich, *A Greek-English Lexicon of the New Testament* (Chicago: University of Chicago Press, 1979), p. 632.

3. C. S. Lewis, *Miracles* (: New York: Collier Books, 1960), pp. 46-47.

4. Jon Meacham, "The Birth of Jesus: From Mary to the manger, how the Gospels mix faith and history to tell the Christmas story and make a case for Christ," *Newsweek,* Atlantic edition, vol. 144, issue 25, December 20, 2004, p. 46.

## Chapter 4: Deity of Christ

1. William Ramsay, quoted in Mark Water, *Hard Questions About the Bible Made Easy* (Peabody, Mass.: Hendrickson Publishers, 2000), p. 11.

2. C. S. Lewis, quoted by Daniel Partner, ed., in *Heroes of the Faith* (Uhrichsville, Ohio: Barbour Publishing, 1998), p. 10.

3. Thomas Watson, quoted in Colin Rowley, ed., "Dogma Dienstag: Is there only one true scripture?" www.noidle brain.com, February 1, 2005.

4. G. K. Chesterton, *Orthodoxy* (New York: Doubleday, 1959), p. 90.

## Chapter 5: Atonement

1. Romans 10:13

## Chapter 6: Resurrection

1. Michael Green, *Man Alive!* (Downers Grove, Ill.: Inter-Varsity Press, 1968), p. 61.
2. Sir Edward Clark, quoted in Lee Strobel, *The Case for Christ* (Grand Rapids, Mich.: Zondervan, 1998), p. 237.

## Chapter 7: Return

1. Thomas Chisholm, "Great Is Thy Faithfulness" (p.d.) *Hymns of the Christian Life* (Harrisburg, Pa.: Christian Publications, Inc., 1936) p. 18.
2. Justin Martyr, *Dialogue with Trypho the Jew.* Christian Classics Ethereal Library, http://www.ccel.org.
3. Clement of Rome, *Second Letter to the Corinthians,* Early Christian Writings, chapter 12. http://www.earlychristian writings.com.

## Chapter 8: The Gospel Stands—No Matter What "They" Say!

1. Michael Hewitt-Gleeson, *Newsell* (Brighton, Victoria, Australia: Wrightbooks, 1990), p. 212.
2. Mark Burnett, quoted in *Outreach* magazine, September/October 2004, p. 17.
3. H. L. Willmington, *That Manuscript from Outer Space* (Nashville: Thomas Nelson, 1977), p. 108.
4. tobyMac on a Public Service Announcement aired on Truth Talk Live radio broadcast. Truth Broadcasting Network (Winston Salem, N.C., June 17, 2005).

5. Evertt Harris, quoted in Dawn Sundstrom, "When God Does Open-Soul Surgery," *Worldwide Challenge*, vol. 25, no. 5, September/October 1998, p.32.

6. V. Raymond Edman quoted in Jennifer Ferranti, "The Road to Hope," Moody Magazine.Com, http://www.moodymagazine.com/articles.php?action=view_article&id=431, June 27, 2005.

7. News Service, "Teens unfamiliar with Bible, poll finds," *Gazette* (Colorado Springs, Colo.), May 1, 2005.

## Chapter 9: Stand

1. Billy Graham, quoted in *The Billy Graham Christian Worker's Handbook* (Minneapolis: World Wide Publications, 1996) p. 237.

2. Katherine Hankey and William G. Fisher (p.d.) *Hymns of the Christian Life,* (Harrisburg, Pa.: Christian Publications, Inc., 1936), p. 240.

3. Billy Graham, quoted in BrainyQuote "Billy Graham quotes," www.brainyquote.com.

4. Nicky Gumbel, *Questions of Life* (Colorado Springs, Colo.: Cook Communications Ministries, 2003), p. 191.

5. Conrad Hilton, *Be My Guest* (New York: Simon & Schuster, 1984), p. 280.

6. Gilbert Keith Chesterton, *Orthodoxy: The Romance of Faith* (New York: Doubleday, 1990), p. 101.

# FOCUS ON THE FAMILY®

*teen outreach*

## At Focus on the Family, we work to help you really get to know Jesus and equip you to change your world for Him.

We realize the struggles you face are different from your parents' or your little brother's, so we've developed a lot of resources specifically to help you live boldly for Christ, no matter what's happening in your life.

Besides teen events and a live call-in show, we have Web sites, magazines, booklets, devotionals, and novels . . . all dealing with the stuff you care about. For a detailed listing of the latest resources, log on to our Web site at **www.go.family.org/teens.**

**Breakaway**
Teen guys
breakawaymag.com

### Focus on the Family Magazines

We know you want to stay up-to-date on the latest in your world — but it's hard to find information on relationships, entertainment, trends, and teen issues that doesn't drag you down. It's even harder to find magazines that deliver what you want and need from a Christ-honoring perspective.

That's why we created *Breakaway* (for teen guys), *Brio* (for teen girls 12 to 16), and *Brio & Beyond* (for girls ages 16 and up). So, don't be left out — sign up today!

**Brio**
Teen girls 13 to 15
briomag.com

**Brio & Beyond**
Teen girls 16 to 19
briomag.com

**Teen Talk Radio**
lifeontheedgelive.com

Phone toll free: (800) A-FAMILY (232-6459)

# *Grow With God*

### Bloom
Need advice on dating and other stuff you're going through? ***Bloom: A Girl's Guide to Growing Up*** is a book you'll return to again and again for honest answers to many of your toughest questions. Sprinkled throughout the book are questions and quizzes that will help you dig deeper into the real you. Find answers about your changing body, dating, guys, sex, and more. Paperback.

### Boom
What's up with my body? Why do I act and think the way I do? Relax. You're not alone. Whether they want to admit it or not, your friends are all asking the same questions. ***Boom: A Guy's Guide to Growing Up*** cuts through the uncertainties of your life and addresses all your questions — body, mind, and soul — transforming you into the confident, godly man you want to be. Paperback.

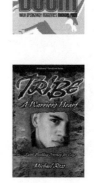

### Tribe
Take your faith to a deeper level. Join the tribe. Deep inside, you yearn for something more. You crave a life of adventure and risk — to be a hero, to be a warrior, to know the Creator intimately. Join the experience in this challenging, 28-day devotional journey that will strengthen your faith and deepen your desire to walk boldly with God! Paperback.

## FOR MORE INFORMATION

**Online:**
Log on to www.family.org

**Phone:**
Call toll free: (800) A-FAMILY

Focus
*on*
*the* Family®